"Words that come from the heart enter into the heart of another."

~ An Iranian Proverb

IN

the *Heart*

OF ANOTHER

IMMIGRANT
WOMEN
TELL THEIR
STORIES

BY *Susan Philips*

AYWN PUBLICATIONS | OREGON

In the Heart of Another: Immigrant Women Tell Their Stories
Copyright © 2009 by Susan Philips

Write to AYWN Publications, 1500 N.E. 15th Avenue #330,
Portland, OR 97232,
or call 503 206 8853 for more information.

Visit our web site at www.aywnpublications.com

ISBN 9781893471177

Library of Congress Control Number: 2009920001

1. Biography   2. Immigrants   3. Women's history

4. Armenia   5. China   6. El Salvador

7. Mexico   8. Vietnam

Published in the United States by AYWN Publications,
1500 N.E. 15th St., #330, Portland, OR 97232

Cover and intro designed by CHERI GRAY / GRAYDESIGN 323 871 8967
Photography by MEENO PELUCE / WWW.MEENOPHOTO.COM
Author Photo by JACOB PINGER

For Mary Lee & Seymour Philips

I dedicate this book to my most enthusiastic cheerleaders, my parents Mary Lee and Seymour (aka Connie Max) Philips, who taught my brothers and me through their words and actions that what defines the worth of a person is not where they're from or what they have or don't have, but rather it is the size of their heart and the generosity of their spirit. ⌐

Table of CONTENTS

Acknowledgments

I have many people to thank. I begin with the eight women I interviewed for the book: Ana, Juanita, María, Michelle, Nara, Oktiabrina, Thuynga and Xidan for their time, their honesty, their humor, and for the trust they placed in me. I thank Fran Caldwell, my editor and publisher, for her friendship, keen eye for detail, and her support for my vision; Meeno Peluce whose photographs are on the cover, and Cheri Gray who designed the front and back covers, for their artistry and heartfelt interest in the project.

I thank Nancy Chen and Jack Trinh, the owners of the Nail Station, a nail salon in Los Angeles, for allowing me to teach English to the Vietnamese and Chinese women who work there. Language is by far and away the most difficult challenge immigrants face when they come to this country. It affects every single part of their lives, from their career choices to their confidence. By providing their employees with an opportunity to learn the language, Nancy and Jack helped give them a brighter future. I encourage other business owners to follow their lead.

I thank all the others who helped along the way: Robin Baltic, Catherine Chang, Dr. Carlos Cortes, Fran Chalin, Mahtash Esfandiari, Gregorio Medina, my husband Art Goldberg, Cyndi V. Huynh, Soledad Jimenez, Manya Lefian, Adam Leipzig, Hector E. Morán, Nguyen Ngoc-Rao, Anthony Pahigian, my son Jacob Pinger, Carolyn Rider, Adele Wallace and Lori Zimmerman.

And finally, like most Americans, I have many family members who have come here from other countries. Their stories are not so different from the ones in this book, and like those women, they have a lot to teach all of us. I begin with my grandparents Sadie and Sam Philips and Elke and Jake Kleiman who came from Russia and Poland, or what they referred to as the "old country," in the early 1900s. Newer arrivals include my niece Rae Chalin from Ukraine, the family of my niece Carmen McDonald from Cuba, my daughter-in-law Karla Alvarado, her mother Martha Cifuentes and their extended family from Guatemala; another daughter-in-law, Munira Virji from Kenya and her family, cousins Anya and Jake Adams from Canada, and Ruth Beaglehole, mother of my stepchildren, from New Zealand.

IN the Heart OF ANOTHER

 FROM LEFT TO RIGHT | María Luisa Onody, Xidan Wang, Nara Movsesian, Ana Leiva, Juanita Leiva, Oktiabrina Osmanian, Michelle Garcia, Thuynga Nguyen.

Introduction

Several years ago after my husband and I moved into our new neighborhood, I did what women everywhere do: I went searching for a place to have my nails done. In Los Angeles, like many other cities across the country, there is no shortage of nail salons. This is due in large part to the thousands of Vietnamese, Korean and Chinese immigrants who have gravitated to these jobs. Each immigrant group that comes to America always seems to find an economic niche. This happens to be one of theirs. Little did I know that this nail salon, and the women who work there, would change my life forever.

The salon was, as my Grandmother Sadie would say, "nothing fancy." The walls, painted a muted white, were broken up by a few randomly placed paintings, like those you find in hotel rooms, and two television sets with the sound almost inaudible. Several bouquets of colorful plastic flowers hung from the walls. A small Buddha surrounded by fresh fruit was the only reminder of the cultural traditions of the people who owned and worked at the salon. Each woman wore a name tag, her American name in large print, pinned to a white smock. When I asked one woman how it felt to have a new name, she said, "My Vietnamese name is hard for Americans to pronounce. Besides, I'm in America now. I need an American name."

Choosing an American name was the easy part; communicating in our language a lot harder. On my weekly visits to the salon, I saw how difficult it was for the women to have a conversation with their customers. Most tried. Some would ask them to speak a little slower. Others would use gestures to make themselves understood or guess at what their customer wanted, which was always dangerous. But no matter how hard the women tried, they would often give up out of frustration or a profound sense of shame and embarrassment. And no matter how much they wanted to learn English, most of the women didn't have the time to go to school. They barely had time to shop, cook, clean and care for their families. Many of the women worked six and even seven days a week, leaving their homes each morning by 7 a.m. and sometimes not returning until 9 p.m. or later when they would eat dinner, relax for a moment and prepare meals for the next day. Despite this, no one complained. "Work is work," they would say. "We have to take care of our family. We have to survive."

This is when I decided to draw upon my experience as a former English-as-a-Second Language (ESL) instructor to teach the women English.

It didn't take long before we established our routine. Once a week at 9 a.m. before the salon opened its doors an hour or so later, I would drive my car into the narrow driveway leading to the parking lot behind the nail salon as the women were getting ready to start their day. Many would be busily eating their breakfast of rice and vegetables mixed with meat or chicken, the one they didn't have time to eat in the mornings while they were getting their kids ready for school. Others would be setting up their stations or cleaning their utensils. At some point, someone would go into the salon to announce that the class was ready to begin, and then one by one my students would come to our makeshift class, notebook in hand, to begin their hour-long lesson. Our classroom, in the parking lot because there was no room in the salon, consisted of several colorful children's plastic chairs arranged in a clumsy circle and covered with a large umbrella to protect us from the sun. I sat in the "big chair," a gray, tattered office chair with wheels that would often roll back into the parking lot if I wasn't careful.

We began each lesson with a "check in," where each woman had an opportunity to talk about anything she wanted. It didn't matter what. My only rule, which was broken pretty much all the time, was that they could use only English. As it turns out, that was a very tall order. But they tried. Some of the women would tell jokes; others would talk about their favorite books and movies, and others would ask me to explain phrases or words they didn't understand. There were a lot of those. One day one of my students asked me to explain the expression, "same old, same old." She asked, "Why would you say the same thing twice?" This made no sense to her. Then, for some reason, every time I asked my students how their week went, they would reply in unison "same old, same old" and howl with laughter. This became our secret joke.

At some point our weekly check-ins began to change. The conversations became more serious and personal. A check-in about love and romance, often a favorite topic, would turn into a discussion about the role of women in their culture. A check-in about their families would turn into a discussion about family members who stayed behind in their countries. And a check-in about what happened at work would turn into a discussion about their careers before coming here, which was for many a painful subject. As I discovered, many of the women had gone to college and established successful careers in their countries. They had been pharmacists, dentists, doctors, nurses or computer programmers. And while they were grateful to America for offering them a safe haven and economic opportunities, they also felt a deep sense of loss for all they had given up.

Slowly, without even knowing it, they were piecing together the stories of their lives. Their stories were often painful, like the time one of the women, a teenager during the Vietnam War, described how she felt the day her father was taken away to a re-education camp, leaving her to care for her younger brothers and sisters while her mother worked at odd jobs to make ends meet. Her childhood ended that day, she said. Current events would trigger memories from home. I can still remember the pained expressions on the faces of the women the day the war in Iraq started as they watched American bombs fall on Baghdad on the television sets. I wondered how it felt to watch a war on a television set after having lived through one. "Americans don't know what it feels like to live through a war in their own country," one of the women said.

By telling me their stories, however sad, however painful, these women were regaining something they had lost when they left their countries and started over in our country—their sense of self. They were letting me know that their lives did not begin when they crossed the border. They had lived a whole other life. They had histories. They had careers. They had families. They had opinions. And they wanted people to know.

And that is why I decided to write this book. I wanted to help these women, and others like them, tell the stories they could not tell by themselves.

I began by asking the women in my class if they wanted to be interviewed. Thuynga, (known in the United States as Tina) from Vietnam and Xidan (known as Linda) from China agreed. Others wanted to participate, but work and family obligations made that impossible. With help from family and friends, I was lucky to find my next interviewees: Maria and her daughter Michelle from Mexico, Ana and her daughter Juanita from El Salvador, and Nara from Armenia. I also interviewed Nara's mother, Oktiabrina. Because of her health, I was not able to spend the time with her I needed to adequately tell her story, but as you will see, when she does speak, her powerful voice and strong opinions jump from the page. She is one tough and smart woman.

After I selected the eight women, we set out together on what was to become a long and emotional journey, one filled with tears, laughter and many losses, theirs and mine. During the three years working on the book, Maria's father developed cancer, and Xidan's and Ana's mothers and my father died. I happened to be with Xidan when her brother called from China with the news of their mother's death. All of the women had told me countless times how painful it was to live so far from home, especially when their families needed them, but it wasn't until that day that I truly understood what that meant. As Xidan told me, "In our culture, children are supposed to be with their parents when they die. I was here. I was a doctor in China. I could have helped." It wasn't lost on me that, unlike Xidan, I was able to be at my father's side when he died.

Along with the sad times, there were many happy times and funny moments. In my mind's eye, I can still see Nara running from her kitchen to her living room or bedroom to find yet another book about Armenian history and culture for me to look at, something she did several times during each interview. One day as she was trying to find room on her table for the three or four new books she was carrying, she stopped in her tracks: "Susan, I think I am giving you too much information. Is that right?" I almost fell out of my chair laughing. What an understatement! Spending time with Nara was like being in school. It made sense. She came to this naturally. She was, after all, a Russian literature and language teacher in Armenia. And it seemed that every time I met with Thuynga, I would ask a question or say something that would make her cry. Sometimes just walking into her house made her cry. This became a running joke. "Susan's here; get the Kleenex." And then there was Michelle's description of her day-long trips on the

Greyhound Bus from Durango to Los Angles and back again where each time she had to sit in the crack between two seats because her mother couldn't afford to buy a third ticket. "Jeans were out of the question," she said, as she demonstrated how she managed to straddle between the two seats. "I always wore sweats." And there was the day when I asked Ana and Juanita if there was any man in their life not named Ricardo. Listing all the important men in her life, Ana confirmed my suspicions. "There are seven," she laughed as she read them off.

We also celebrated everything we possibly could, including important holidays like Chinese and Vietnamese New Year's, Christmas, the days marking the Armenian Genocide and the Chinese Revolution, and more personal celebrations like weddings and birthdays. I was even invited to a surprise baby shower for Ana's first grandchild. I was the first guest to arrive and waited for at least an hour for the other guests to arrive on "Salvadoran time." What was I thinking? But I did get to help Juanita decorate the patio with dozens of little babies she had spent hours making for her new niece. Of the 100 or so guests who came, 90 percent were family. As Juanita told me, "It seems like half of the world are my cousins." Everyone lives close by; and unlike American culture, everyone is in each other's lives on a daily basis. There is no concept of privacy, none whatsoever. Their home, like those of all the women I interviewed, is always open to family and friends. No questions asked.

And their homes were also opened to me. There was never a time when I wasn't greeted with warmth, open arms, and on many occasions, delicious food. As in my Jewish family, food plays a huge part in their lives, and, as I learned, you can never refuse to eat. "You must try everything," Nara would say. And so I did. I ate noodle soups from China, moon cakes from Vietnam, tamales from Mexico, soups and an assortment of nuts, candies and preserves from Armenia. Then in what became our ritual, we would fill each other in on the details of our lives between interviews as we pushed away all the stuff that clutters kitchen tables everywhere, regardless of culture—dishes, mail, napkins, and lots of tchochkas (the Yiddish word for lots of little things) to make room for my tape recorder, tapes and batteries before beginning the work at hand. Ana and Juanita won first prize for the most tchochkas. In their kitchen and den, dolls, salt and pepper shakers, toothpick holders and plates, just to mention a few, are displayed with care in every conceivable space, literally taking over both rooms. As Juanita explained, "This is called the 'horror of emptiness.' We don't want to leave any space unfilled."

This was true to a lesser extent with the other women. In Xidan's apartment, colorful flowers of all sorts are everywhere. Small pink, yellow and white artificial flowers drape across walls and hang from light fixtures; and paper flowers fill large Chinese vases that sit on the floor. "Chinese people love flowers," Xidan told me. If we don't have real ones, artificial ones will do." In Nara's small kitchen, pictures of bright red pomegranates, a favorite Armenian fruit, hang above the door that separates the kitchen from the living room; plates and baskets of all shapes and sizes from all over the world fill her kitchen walls; and family photographs and books are pretty much everywhere.

Now it's time for you to meet these eight women. Find a comfortable chair and sit down at your kitchen table. Put on a pot of coffee or herbal tea (hey, I'm from California), and try to imagine that these women are sitting across the table from you, as they were from me. They will talk about the things that matter to them: their lives, cultures, and families. They will explain why they left their homes and describe the challenges of adjusting to a new country. And with the clarity that comes from being "an outsider," they will offer insights into the culture and values of America as they reflect on their own.

I leave you with one final thought. The women in these stories do not want either your praise or your pity. They do not think of themselves as heroes or their stories heroic. They think of themselves as survivors who did what they had to do to take care of their families. Nothing more; nothing less. As Thuynga told me during her final interview, "Don't think of me as special. My story is a common one. Some people had it harder; others had it easier. What happened to me happened to a lot of other people."

Susan Philips

Nara's and Oktiabrina's Stories

Nara Movsesian was born in Erevan, the capital of Armenia, on April 17, 1958. Before coming to the United States, Nara was a Russian language and literature teacher for fourteen years. She came to the United States on May 28, 1992, following her husband, Souren, who came a year earlier. Initially, Souren was very excited about the many changes that took place in Armenia after the country declared its independence from the Soviet Union, but when he saw that the new bureaucracy and government were becoming too corrupt and any resistance to the system was becoming dangerous, he felt he had no choice but to leave. Nara's mother, Oktiabrina, and father, Rafik, joined Nara in 1993. Here are Nara's and Oktiabrina's stories.

Nara

Nara and Oktiabrina share a moment, 2008.

Historical Note:

The Armenian people have a long and painful history. At various times, they have suffered invasions by Romans, Persians, Byzantines, Mongols, Arabs and Ottoman Turks. The saddest chapter in their history occurred between 1915 and 1922 at the hands of the Ottoman Empire and is known as the Armenian Genocide. On April 24, 1915, the ruling political party within the Ottoman state (present-day Turkey), The Committee for Union and Progress, began a program of ethnic cleansing against their Armenian neighbors. Fueled by a racist-nationalist ideology, the Young Turks, as they were called, eventually slaughtered over one and a half million Armenian people.

Despite continued international pressure and overwhelming historical proof, Turkey has to this day failed to recognize the fact of the Armenian Genocide. The attempted genocide created a diaspora (diaspora is a Greek word meaning a scattering of seeds), forcing millions of Armenians to settle in Central Asia, the Middle East, Europe and the United States.

After Turkey was defeated in World War I, Armenia claimed its independence on May 28, 1918, but independence was to last only two short years. In 1920, the country was annexed by the Soviet Union. Two years later, the Soviets placed Georgia, Armenia and Azerbaijan in what was called the Transcaucasia Soviet Socialist Republic.

Erevan has been the capitol of Armenia since the country gained its independence in 1918. The largest city in the country, today it has a population of over one million.

My Mother's Family

My grandmother, Lusik Osmanian, was born in the city of Izmir, Turkey, in 1903. During World War I, she escaped with her grandmother Ovsanna to Nakhichevan, a city in the Russian part of Armenia. Her parents stayed in Izmir, and she never saw them again. When my grandmother was thirteen, the family arranged a marriage for her to an eighteen-year-old Armenian boy. He was tall, handsome and very masculine, but my grandmother was shy, and whenever her new husband tried to talk to her, she would take cover behind her mother-in-law.

World War I was still in progress when her young husband left to serve in the army. This was a difficult time for my grandmother. While her husband was gone, she developed typhus and was hospitalized for a long time. With nowhere else to go, she went back to live with her mother-in-law, who viewed her as just another mouth to feed in a time of hunger. Then one winter day while trying to keep warm, my grandmother accidentally caught her feet in a toundir (a large hole in the ground used for baking) and burned her legs so badly that she had to spend another year in the hospital.

Nara's mother's grandmother, Ovsanna (center), with great-uncle and aunt, Tigran and Miranousch, in Rostov, Russia, early 1900s.

7

Her husband never came back from the war, and she never heard what happened to him.

When my grandmother was twenty-four, her relatives took her to live in Erevan, where she met my grandfather, Pogos Osmanian, who was twenty years older. He was fifty years old when my mother, Oktiabrina, was born. My mother tells me that my grandmother was an angel. The neighbors were crazy about her and always came to ask for her advice. She was trusting with a child's innocence. People used to say, "If you give her a stone, you can take bread from her." When she passed away, everyone cried.

I didn't know my mother's father because he died when I was one year old. I know that he was born in 1880 in the city of Shamakhi, which is currently in the territory of Azerbaijan. When he was older, he moved to Baku and became involved in the Bolshevik Revolution. He was very dedicated to the high ideals and morals of the revolution. Like everyone, my grandfather was excited about the new independent and fair country where people would be equal, free and happy, and where there would be no more poverty. It was a euphoric time. Everyone thought that things would be better after the revolution. They said, "We are struggling now; we are poor and hungry; many mistakes are being made around us, but things will be better." Ironically when World War II came, people thought the same thing, "Things will be better after the war." But this never happened. When the Soviet soldiers visited East Germany a decade after the war, they were shocked to find the defeated former enemy prospering while the conquering Soviet Union was still struggling for a better future.

My grandfather's dedication to the Bolshevik Revolution was extreme. Many communist families had what was called "red baptisms" where they gave their kids communist names, like Proletariat. He named my mother Oktiabrina, which means October, the month the revolution started. He named my aunts and uncles Karlen (Karl Marx and Vladimir Lenin), Lena (Lenin), Vladimir (Vladimir Lenin) and Robert after Robert Power, who was a revolutionary from Germany.

Historical Note:
The Bolshevik Revolution, also known as the October Revolution, took place in Russia on October 25, 1917, and was followed by a civil war creating the Union of Soviet Socialist Republics, also known as the Soviet Union, in 1922. The Bolsheviks were a political party founded by Vladimir Lenin, who became the first head of the Soviet Union and the originator of Leninism, a branch of Marxist communist theory.

Leon Trotsky was a comrade of Lenin and a fellow leader of the October Revolution. After Lenin's death, Trotsky was forcibly expelled from the Communist Party for leading the Left Opposition, a movement that opposed Joseph Stalin's rise to power. Trotsky was deported and eventually assassinated by Stalinist agents in Mexico. His political theories are known as Trotskyism and his followers as Trotskyites.

Because he was active in the Communist Party and had good management skills, my grandfather was sent to Krasnodar to become the manager of a large factory where they printed money. Everybody was checked for stolen cash when they left the factory at the end of each day, but nobody checked my grandfather because of his impeccable reputation for honesty.

In 1937, my grandfather was accused of being a Trotskyite and taken to jail. This was very difficult for the family. Since my grandmother was a housewife and the children were still young, they relied on him to bring bread to the family. Everybody from his work was shocked about his arrest because they knew how dedicated he was to the Communist Party. Many went to the Central Committee to speak on his behalf. "How can you accuse him?" they said. He was released after two months when the uncle of one of his supporters, who was the judge of the city, told the authorities that my grandfather had been falsely accused. My grandfather was so physically and emotionally beaten by his arrest and imprisonment that he left his Communist Party membership card on the table of the communist authorities. The party secretary tried to talk him out of resigning, but my grandfather told them, "After all I have done for the party, you have offended me. Now I see what's going on, and I will never sit at the same table with these corrupt people. These are not real Bolsheviks; these are not the people with whom I fought for communist ideals." It was a miracle how he stayed alive after what he had said about the party officials.

My Father's Family

My father's side came from the city of Van in Turkey, which was one of the ancient capitals of Armenia. Armenians from Van suffered relatively less during the Genocide than Armenians from other cities in Turkey because they were able to organize an active resistance movement. Two other areas did the same thing. One was Musa Dagh, a large mountainous village at the shore of the Mediterranean Sea, whose population escaped by French ship. The other was Sassoun.

Van was a very rich and prosperous city with many schools, colleges, and foreign missions. The people were hard workers from different social classes: merchants, jewelers, lawyers, doctors, priests. My father's family was rich, and like many Armenians, they were good merchants. One of the main characteristics of Armenians from Van is that they know how to make money, and most important, how to save money. One of the most popular jokes about Armenians from Van is that in the morning instead of greeting each other and wishing a good morning, they ask, "How much yellow today (gold on the market)?"

During the Genocide, my grandfather (Khazar Gulnazarian) had many tragedies. His first wife was killed by the Turks in front of his eyes, and as he was fleeing with his small daughter, he lost her in the chaos. He never found her. He hoped that she had become an American orphan because during the Genocide many American missionaries took babies back to America. My grandfather was fortunate in that he was able to hide some gold and jewelry in the hems and collars of his clothes, which allowed him to survive.

His second wife, my grandmother (Nubar Iskandarian), also had a big tragedy. Her first husband was killed during the Genocide. She was able to flee with her three-year-old daughter Maro, but as they were escaping, one of the Turks threw Maro to the ground and stabbed her with his sword. It was a miracle that

The Armenian Genocide caused a huge pain.
This pain comes from the milk of our mothers.
This is part of our existence.

she survived because they didn't have any ointment or remedy to give her. With no other option, my grandmother tied Maro's skin together with a thread. When Auntie Maro was older, we would always ask to see her wound.

During their escape, my grandfather and grandmother met and got married. Eventually they had four children together, my father and my three aunts. When my grandparents entered the city of Erevan with the thousands of other Armenians who were fleeing the Genocide, they saw huge orchards. They were so hungry they started eating all the fruits as fast as they could. Many people developed dysentery and half of them died. Can you imagine? They escaped the Turks but died in Armenia from poverty and sickness? Among the thousands of Armenians who escaped the Turkish Massacre was the family of Arshile Gorky, the founder of abstract expressionism in the United States, but sadly his mother also died from hunger. Gorky felt huge pain over this for his entire life.

It is impossible to find an Armenian family that didn't suffer. The Armenian Genocide caused a huge pain. This pain comes from the milk of our mothers. This is part of our existence. One and one-half million Armenians were killed, and we are still trying to tell people that the Genocide happened. Even now the government of Turkey refuses to accept what happened and continues to manipulate the historical events.

Around 1970, the Soviet government finally built a memorial recognizing the Genocide. Until this time, we weren't able to talk openly about it. People were afraid of being accused of nationalism. Everybody was Soviet. The idea of communism was that everybody was equal and everybody was fighting for one country, one idea. You could not think about yourself or your nation; you had to think about everybody in the society. We were told: "We are Soviet people. We are building a new era." The Soviet Union also did not want to spoil a good relationship with their neighbor, Turkey.

I can remember one time when I was about ten years old. My father had picked me up at school, and when we got home and opened the mailbox, there was a photograph of the Ararat Mountains surrounded with chains. Slaughtered and murdered Armenians encircled the mountain. This was the symbol of the wounded and enslaved motherland. This was a picture of the Genocide.

There was a question on the photograph: How long will it take before people will accept the Genocide? I asked my father, "What is this?" My father crumpled up the paper, put it in his pocket and responded, "It is nothing. Let's go home." You never knew what would happen to you if someone from the ruling party or KGB found you with the photo. My life and the history of my country are deeply connected with the Genocide.

> *Historical Note:*
> *The KGB was the Russian political security police force. Created in 1954, the unit functioned as an espionage agency as well as a means to fight against internal subversion and domestic dissidence.*

My Parents

My mother, Oktiabrina, was born on September 10, 1923, in Krasnodar. She was the oldest of three sons and two daughters, and because of her mother's poor health, she had to care for the home and the family. Despite that, she finished high school with a gold medal for "honors" and passed the exam to go to the university. My mother was beautiful, hardworking and smart. She always dreamed about becoming a doctor, but when my father came back from World War II, he told her that it was either him or the university. He thought that if she went to the university, she would never marry him, and because my mother loved him so much, she chose my father over her dream. Eventually, she became a registered nurse. She did this work for over fifty years.

Nara's mother, Oktiabrina, in Erevan, 1960s.

My mother was afraid that because I was an only child I might become a selfish person. If I took an apple, my mom would say, "Are you going to eat that by yourself? Did you ask your father if he wanted any? Did you ask me?" I am thankful for that. She taught me to be a good, sharing person and not to think about just myself. She is also pathologically honest. If I told her I had bought something for $3, she would correct me, "Why are you giving the wrong information? You bought this for $2.97." Her honesty genetically came from her father.

Nara's father on the right as a soldier at the Russian Front, 1941-42.

My father, Rafik, was born on March 15, 1922, in Erevan. He was very smart and alert but was also audacious and romantic, and sometimes he would lie down on the balcony and watch the clouds move and change their shape. My mom and dad were schoolmates. They had studied several years in the same high school. Both were very well known in the school, but for different reasons. My mother was neat, organized and always prepared to answer the most difficult questions. She was a passionate leader and participant in all school events. She was a dream student. My father, on the other hand, was well known as one of the troublemakers in the school. He would always make noise, laugh and make a fuss. When my mother would see my father in the school lobby, she would walk the other way to avoid saying "hello." Then one day everyone was in the sports hall except my mom. She was standing in front of an open window singing a song. When she finished, she turned back and saw my father looking at her with admiration. She hadn't noticed when he entered the room. "You sing beautifully," he said. At that moment, the love story of my mom and dad began.

My father told me many stories about his early life. When he was growing up, Erevan was going from a provincial town with a poor infrastructure to a modern city. From morning to night, you would see barefoot boys selling drinking water in ceramic jugs. There was a huge competition between the boys to see who could sell the most water. You could hear sounds of their voices everywhere, "Cold water, cold water from the fountains." There is a monument of a skinny boy proudly carrying a jug of water in one of the central alleys in Erevan. My father used to joke. "This is me when I was in the water-selling business."

My father was a very brave person and an authority among his friends. One day before the start of World War II, an officer from the KGB told him that they

High school photo, 1941. Nara's father is in the middle of the first row, and her mother is second from the left in the back.

were planning on sending him to spy school. When my father told my grandfather about this, my grandfather said, "It would be better that my son would be killed than for him to cause the death of other people's children." My father refused this assignment, and he was sent instead to the general army. He was seventeen years old.

When my father was twenty-one and wounded from the war, he returned home and went to work as a laborer in a textile factory. He eventually became one of the managers of the largest departments in the factory, and for twenty-five years, he was the secretary of the Communist Party at the factory. At that time in the Soviet Union, every business, factory, school and farm had to have a secretary of the Communist Party. I don't think he really believed in the party, but he was a good organizer and used his ability to help people. He was able to get a lot of benefits for the laborers. He was a kind, fair, independent and principled manager.

My father had a huge influence on my character and personality. My love of nature, art and books comes from my father. Sometimes we even fought about who would read the new books first. He was also an Erevan guy (Erevantsi), and when we would walk

Nara's father, Rafik, in Erevan, in his forties.

13

through the city, he would tell me stories about all the historical buildings and the people who lived in them. He was in love with his country.

He admired Nikita Khrushchev for freeing a million Soviet people from the hell of the GULAG. I remember one time when I was about sixteen, my father and I visited Moscow. He took me to the place where Krushchev was buried. The grave was in terrible condition. My father was very angry about this because he respected Khrushchev so much.

My Life Growing Up

My generation lived during the best time of the Soviet Union. We lived as though in a fairy tale, feeling happy and safe. We grew up with the best human values like sharing and friendship. I had ev-

erything I needed, but not in large quantities. Now I have a closet full of shoes, but I think I need a new pair because we are getting another type of brainwashing: buy, buy, buy. Where is the middle ground between socialism and capitalism, materialism and idealism?

Everyone got a strong academic education. Students could not work at a job; they had to study. The government also believed that all kids should have an arts education, which was almost free. I studied the piano for eight years. We grew up on the books of great international writers such as Cooper, Fitzgerald, Hemingway, Balzac, Kafka, Chekhov, Tolstoy, Dostoevsky, Pushkin, Gorky, and others. Festivals, concerts, movies and theatrical performances were so popular that it was difficult sometimes to find tickets.

My mom made sure that I got a Russian education. My father read and spoke perfect Russian, but my mom suffered because she didn't. Russian was the common language for all republics in the Soviet Union. If you wanted a better future, you needed to be a communist with good Russian language skills.

We saw things through rose-colored glasses.

I grew up thinking that the United States was the biggest enemy to the Soviet Union. The United States was where rich people tortured poor people, where black people suffered. When I was ten or eleven years old, I remember how impressed I was by the movie *Circus* by a famous filmmaker named Grigori Aleksandrov, one of Stalin's favorite directors. In his movies, most of which were musicals, he showed Soviet life in an embellished way. You couldn't wish for better propaganda.

Circus is about a young American woman working in the circus who has a son with a black man. When she comes to the Soviet Union, the Soviet people don't care that her son is black, whereas the Americans had wanted to blacklist her. She falls in love with a Russian guy. The movie shows the difficulties of her situation and how unfair things were for black people in the United States. In the movie, people from the circus march through Red Square singing the following song. It was one of the most popular songs during Soviet rule.

These are the words they sang:

"This dear land, the land of our motherland,

Offers a gift more precious than precious gems.

There is no country on Earth that is richer or more beautiful;

Everyone feels they are free.

One man is worth as much as any other,

Whether brown-skinned or white,

They all agree because men are equal,

And they are worth as much as the work they perform."

Unconsciously, we knew that this was not the full story. We knew that things were better in the United States. There was a joke: "Yes capitalism would die, but the smell would be perfect." We saw how the United States prospered. When people went to the United States for trips, they came back with nice stuff. We knew there were problems with our country as well. There was no freedom of speech. We could not organize demonstrations. We saw things through rose-colored glasses. While one part of the society was singing this song, the other part was exiled, beaten, tortured, murdered without any reason by brainwashed

Nara is in the middle with cousins Gayane on the left and Ninel on the right, 1964-65.

"human beings." It is terrible to think about how we were lied to and how dangerous life was for many people. We didn't find out about the twenty million people in Siberia who were killed until after the collapse of the Soviet Union.

I Become a Teacher

After graduating from high school, I attended Erevan State Linguistic University to become a teacher of Russian language and literature. I love kids, and I love literature. For Armenians, education is the most important thing. It is the basis of our prosperity. If you have a good education, everyone will respect you. Parents are obsessed with their kids' education. They could be hungry, but their kids will get a good education. There are stories that during the Genocide some women saved books they had taken from the churches by hiding them in their clothing. Our strength is in our knowledge.

The university I attended was named after Valery Bryusov, a well-known Russian poet, prose writer, translator, historian and critic of the Russian Literature of the Silver Age. He played a significant role in the popularization of Armenian poetry during the time of the ordeals of 1915 when Armenians were on the verge of extermination. The years in university were among the happiest times in my life. I studied hard but always had time to attend concerts, take vacations, and go to picnics and parties.

Every new teacher in the Soviet Union was required to teach in a province for at least two years. I was sent to work in Charentsavan, a town located in the northern part of Armenia. Most of the people in the town were repatriates from

Iran. Almost none could speak Russian, so it was difficult for the kids to get help from their parents. Also, because most of the parents had already decided to move to the United States as quickly as possible, they didn't think their kids needed to learn Russian.

After World War II, thousands of Armenians from Iran and other countries, like Greece, Lebanon, Syria, Egypt and France, returned to Armenia with the hope that they would be able to build a free new motherland. But there were problems. Armenia was a big disappointment for them. They were nostalgic about their motherland, but because it was communistic, they could not own property or businesses. They felt they had to escape to the United States. Since at that time I was Soviet Armenian, I thought the Armenians who were leaving were traitors.

After seven years of working in Charentsavan, I found a teaching job at a school that was walking distance from my house in Erevan. God was so merciful. The school was named after the Armenian writer Perch Proshian. The students came from poor families from the countryside. Like all societies, Armenia had people from different economic levels, but it was generally pretty even, and people with money didn't show it as much as they do here.

My classroom looked out on the Ararat Mountains, which throughout the centuries has been a national symbol of Armenia. Ararat is a beautiful mountain with two peaks, covered year-round with snow. The view is breathtaking. Armenian literature, songs, restaurants, streets, towns, and even the name of a soccer team carry the name of that legendary mountain. Although now Ararat is located on the Turkish side, it remains in the heart of each and every Armenian.

Number 15, Perch Proshian School in the 1980s in Erevan.
Nara is the teacher with the white blouse in the second row.

A view of the Ararat Mountains, which are mentioned in the Bible. The city of Erevan is in the foreground.

I taught students from the first grade through high school. In Armenian schools, students study the Russian language for ten years. In elementary classes, students study Russian five hours a week, and then gradually in middle and high school, the hours became fewer and fewer. I tried to give my students a good base of knowledge of the Russian language and demanded that they learn this. We learned together and we grew up together. I knew everything about them. One of the important elements of my teaching was to connect students with the arts and nature. If the mind and soul of kids are not filled with these things, sooner or later negative influences will force them to take one wrong step after another. When your soul is rich, it helps you survive.

I also tried to teach my students to be civil and sensitive to people and to the world, modest and open-minded. Chekhov, my favorite writer, in a letter to his brother, wrote that an intelligent person is not a person who knows how to use the right fork or knife but is a person who never notices when one of the guests spills sauce on the tablecloth.

Historical Note:
The mountains of Ararat are located between the Black and Caspian Seas in southern Armenia. The King James Bible refers to them in the story of Noah's Ark: "At the end of a hundred and fifty days the waters had abated; and in the seventh month, on the seventeenth day of the month, the ark came to rest upon the mountains of Ararat." (Genesis 8:1-4) The higher of the two peaks was known to the ancient Persians as "Noah's Mountain."

Marrying Souren

I knew Souren from childhood because we lived in the same building and on the same floor. We fell in love when I was twenty-five, and we married when I was twenty-seven, which was a little unusual because most girls in Armenia get married earlier than I did. Everyone was surprised when we started dating because we had been friends for so long. He is a dream husband, very devoted and tender. I send him to buy bread, and he comes back with flowers. I like this craziness. People need to be a bit crazy. I fell in love with him because he was very smart and hard-working. After he graduated as an economist, he headed the Department of Sociological Research in Erevan City Hall.

Our married life started on December 25, 1985. Instead of a wedding party, we decided we'd rather have a beautiful honeymoon. My honeymoon was a fairy tale. I will remember it for the rest of my life. We went to Leningrad, which is now called St. Petersburg. There we went to a ballet called *The Citizens of Kale* at the Mariinski Theatre. In the foyer of our hotel, we saw Marcello Mastroianni, a well-known Italian artist, and Nikita Mikhalkov, a Russian director. Everybody was shocked seeing Mastroianni in person. In the 1980s he was an idol all over the world. He wore a white hat and long white coat. People were yelling his name, "Mastroianni, Mastroianni." We spent a gorgeous New Year's Eve at the restaurant at the Astoria Hotel where we were staying. When the people realized that we had just gotten married, they threw raisins, rice

In our culture, kids and old people are the holy people.

and money at us, symbols of prosperity. It was noisy and funny, with music and people. In the morning there was total silence. It was snowing. It was silent and snowing. I felt so happy.

We wanted to have children but we couldn't. Not having a child has been a big unhappiness for me, my husband and my parents. In our culture, kids and old people are the holy people. We are a loving couple, but deep in our hearts, something very important is missing. Armenians are family-oriented, and having a child is important. A family without kids is like a church without bells. We have a saying, "A man is a man if he puts trees in the ground, builds a house and has a child." My father suffered until the day he died from the idea of not having any grandkids. The month before he died he said to me, "Tell me that you are pregnant." I could not lie to him. He looked at me sadly. This is the mentality. Grandparents want to take care of their grandkids. He was worried that he would not be able to transfer all his wisdom and knowledge to them.

War with Azerbaijan over Nagorno-Karabakh

Historical Note:

The period 1988-1994 brought war and destruction to Armenia. In 1988, Armenia and Azerbaijan began a six-year war over a region in Azerbaijan called Nagorno-Karabakh, a largely Armenian area under the jurisdiction of Azerbaijan. As part of its war strategy, Azerbaijan set up a blockade preventing food, oil and natural gas from entering Armenia. Turkey, an ally of Azerbaijan, closed its border as well, further crippling the Armenian economy and infrastructure.

Later that same year, Armenia was hit by a 6.9 magnitude earthquake, killing over 25,000 people and injuring another 15,000. While Erevan was not hit hard, the city of Spitak was almost totally destroyed and the cities of Leninakan, Stepanavan and Kirovakan suffered severe damage. Three years later, the war with Azerbaijan still raging, the Armenian legislature declared Armenia's independence. On Christmas Day 1991, the Soviet Union collapsed.

These were the worst years for Armenia. The earth and Karabakh were collapsing at the same time. It was like the Genocide. The economic situation was unbearable. Azerbaijan and Turkey had closed their borders with Armenia, which meant that almost nothing could get through to the people. Only the borders with Georgia and Iran were open, but they were very small. The economy was collapsing all around us. Industrial centers were closed. People couldn't work. There was no heavy industry; there was no light industry. There was no transportation. Everything was shut down. Erevan was like a dead city.

Life was terrible. We had light one hour a day and water two hours a day. One day I would wash the top of my body and the next day the other half. Every cup of water was counted. When I moved here to the United States, every time I took a shower I told myself, "I know why I am here, to take a shower." We had no food. In Armenia there was always something on our table, but during this time, we didn't have anything on the table. You had to think only about yourself. It was so cold, we slept in our coats. People cut trees in the park to use for heat. Schools remained open, but we had to cut the hours because there was no heat in the classrooms, and kids couldn't study at home because they didn't have light. But through it all, the symphonic orchestra continued to perform. The government tried to keep the ticket prices low so people could come. It was a little warmer in the opera building.

The winter of 1992 was the coldest winter ever. I missed most of this because I had already come to the United States, but my parents were still in Armenia. I worried all the time. I cried all year. Every Armenian had someone in Armenia, but it was almost impossible to get food to them. We were lucky because my cousin, Anahit, in Moscow was able to send my parents and her parents food every day. Without the Diaspora, no one would have survived. Like one of our prime ministers said, "Some people have oil, we have the Diaspora."

Throughout our history, everyone tried to kill us and we survived. During the Ottoman Empire, we were subdued. The Turks tried to take away our pride. They wanted us to forget that we were Armenian. They would cut out our tongues when we wanted to speak Armenian. Nothing can destroy us. We are survivors, and we want the world to know that we are here.

> *Nothing can destroy us. We are survivors, and we want the world to know that we are here.*

Independence

The collapse of the Soviet Union happened gradually. No country could ever conquer the Soviet Union. The fall had to come from within. People couldn't live like this anymore. Problems were always there. The economy was horrible, and once Gorbachev started his political reforms, it was impossible to stop what happened. People wanted their freedom. This started with Karabakh and spread to the Baltic areas. Empires always collapse.

I felt proud that we were free and independent, but it was very expensive. The price was very high. We paid with our misery. Our good feelings about independence were covered by the economic problems. We were a new country, but we were in a terrible condition. Nothing worked. Prices were down. Shrewd, pragmatic people bought steel, diamonds, oil and forests for very little. These were the same people who had been undercover capitalists before the Soviet Union collapsed. We saw beggars. We had never seen beggars before. We saw people eating out of trash cans. People lost their apartments. A lot of old people lost their homes. Some people thought that we were better off under the Soviet Union. Everything was happening so quickly. People didn't have time to change their consciousness.

Initially, Souren was very excited about all the changes taking place. It was a new era with more freedom. Everything was fresh. He had a good job in Erevan City Hall as the manager of the Department of Sociological Research. He was trying to make things fairer, but gradually he began to see corruption

Historical Note:
Mikhail Gorbachev served as head of the Soviet Union from 1985 until 1991. His economic reforms, known as perestroika, *and freedom of information policies, known as* glasnost, *contributed to the end of the Cold War with the United States and eventually to the dissolution of the Soviet Union.*

setting in. People were protecting their friends, giving them the good jobs, the same things he saw under the Soviet system. He came to believe that the system would never change. When he realized that it would never change, he knew he couldn't live there any longer.

Coming to the United States

I didn't come to the United States because I wanted to. I came because my husband Souren came. We didn't know what life would be like here. People who came here never talked about the difficult things. Complaining is not in the Armenian character. Maybe they were ashamed. I thought maybe I would come here for one year to be with him and then go back. I couldn't imagine myself without Armenia. I was a city girl from Erevan. I had such a wonderful life in Armenia. I loved everything—my city, my library, my music, my piano, my parents, my work, my home, my friends.

The day I left was terrible. Part of my heart was happy because I was going to see my husband, but another part cried because I was leaving my parents. As an only child, I was very attached to my parents. All my friends and relatives gathered in my home and then brought me to the airport. I remember how my father and mother sat on a bench as though they were lost. They didn't know if this was the last time they would see me. I thought, "Oh my god, am I going to see them again?" I had a friend who was an artist who drew two portraits of me. One I liked and the other I didn't. I left the best one because I knew I would be back.

When Souren arrived in the United States, he moved in with his cousin, and then shortly before I came, he rented an apartment for us. His friends all helped him fix it up. They brought everything he needed: sofa, television, vacuum,

Nara and her husband, Souren, in Los Angeles, 1996.

22

bedding, blankets, pots and pans. It was such a nice and cozy apartment, I was shocked when I saw it. That is how we do things. Armenian people always think about each other. We help each other. We need each other. This is how we have survived.

My first impression of the United States was two huge metallic rivers running opposite each other. These were the freeways. Another memory is a street of one-story houses side by side with their lonely, naked palm trees under the burning sun. No shade. When we had imagined the United States, we thought about busy, noisy streets with skyscrapers. But the street where I lived looked like the countryside. I was used to the city. This impression stayed with me until Souren showed me the downtown area with modern architecture, sculptures, fountains and, of course, traffic. I wanted to enjoy each part of the city. But it was shocking to see rich areas of the city so close to other parts built out of ragged boxes, with people living in unbearable conditions. The contrast between wealth and poverty was abnormal.

Historical Note:
The Armenian community in the United States has grown considerably in the course of the last century. The largest wave of immigration came after World War II when 700,000 Armenians immigrated to Europe or the United States. The U.S. Census Bureau estimates about 60,000 Armenians came to the United States between 1969 and 1980. Most settled in California, particularly in and around Los Angeles. In the 2000 U.S. Census Report, 26.2 percent of Glendale, California's population identified themselves as Armenian.

The year I was in Erevan without Souren, I felt lonely, but the beginning months here with my husband near to me, I felt lonelier. My uncertain future made me depressed. Throughout my life, I had worked or studied. I didn't know what my occupation would be here. I cried every day. I didn't know the language. For me, every day without information or news was like living in a vacuum. For the first year, every day I thought I would go back to Armenia. I thought this was just temporary. But when my parents came, I knew it was not temporary. It would be a huge problem to take them back.

At first my father refused to come to the United States, but my mother told him that she was coming, that she would die without her daughter. It was difficult for her to leave because she thought she would never be able to come back. Her whole life was in Armenia. My father forbade her from bringing anything with her because he planned to come back after a few months. He thought he would see me and then go back.

When my mother arrived in Los Angeles, she was disappointed. Like me, she thought it would be like New York, but it was more like the countryside. She missed Erevan, the Armenian trees, the people, the air, everything, but especially the trees. She said, "My heart is in Armenia, but my body is here." She worried all the time about what was going on there. She had one wish for Armenia—that the government would go away and young, smart, educated people would run the country.

Every day my father thought about going back. We could be eating dinner and he would take seeds from his food, put them in a napkin and save them for his orchard back in Armenia. He always thought about his orchard. I promised to buy him the best seeds in the United States. He waited for his green card, but it never arrived. One day he realized that he would never go back and he collapsed. My father died in 1998, five years after he and my mom came here.

At his funeral, our friend wrote of my father. "There is comfort in knowing that he is no longer suffering. The only sadness comes from knowing that he died in a foreign land. Here was a veteran who'd survived the Battle of Stalingrad as a seventeen-year-old Armenian soldier newly conscripted into the Soviet Army, fighting the combined forces of fascism. His family's only regret is that he was never able to see his beloved Armenia again, or to cast his eyes on the sun setting behind Mount Ararat, or to walk through his fruit orchard, inhaling the sweet fragrance of the persimmon and apricot blossoms."

Working in America

My first job was at a sewing factory. I can describe that time of my life in one word: slavery. After I got my work permit, I went to work in a Beverly Hills hotel in the housekeeping department. It was so humiliating for me to see the private lives of people I didn't know. I paid a lot physically and emotionally in this job. I was suffering every moment.

I needed to tell everyone—I am not that person you think I am. I can do more than housekeeping.

I cleaned thirteen or fourteen rooms each day and earned maybe $7.25 an hour. Every day on my way home from work, I would decide to quit, but the reality of my life sent me back again and again. "Why am I here? Why did God punish me and change my life?" Then I would answer, "You came here voluntarily; it is nobody's fault. Your English and qualifications are so limited." I was desperate. I cried on the way to work. I cried on the way from work. After work, I went to school to study English three nights a week. This was in addition to my work, shopping, cooking, and taking care of my parents. At night I was so exhausted. I was just running all the time. I didn't exist.

Then something good happened. Close to Christmas, the management organized a Christmas party and asked if there was anyone who could accompany the choir on the piano. I offered my help. I needed to tell everyone—I am not that person you think I am. I can do more than housekeeping. They must have thought "How could this housekeeper who can hardly understand English be a musician?" But they were desperate. They needed somebody and decided to give me a try. During the week I found the music for the Christmas carols and began practicing with the choir. It was my time! I enjoyed every moment of these practices. Office workers from the management and receptionists, who had every day looked at me without noticing me, surrounded me around the piano, trying to sing properly under my direction. During this time I was thankful for my stubborn mom who made me practice the piano.

Nara playing the piano at the hotel Christmas party.

Finally it was Christmas Eve. There I was in this huge hall playing the piano for the choir. My heart was full of happiness, and I felt so much pride. After the performance, one of the corporate people approached our table and asked permission to join us. He couldn't understand how someone from the housekeeping department was able to play the piano and lead a chorus. That was my happiest day in the United States. They had never noticed me before. Here a person without language is looked at as a stupid person, a dummy. People look at you but they don't really see you.

When I thought my language was good enough, I went to work at Robinsons-May Department Store and then Nordstrom. I have worked at Nordstrom for ten years, the first eight in the accessory department and the last two in the handbag department. Every day I see a huge, colorful gallery of people from all over the country and all over the world, from Europe, Vietnam, China and Arabic countries. Every day I am learning something new by talking with my customers and co-workers.

My Mother and I Visit Armenia

In September of 2006, my mom and I went back to Armenia. I had strange feelings. I had known Erevan all my life. Every block was full of memories. My heart was screaming, ''Hello, my city, do you remember me?'' I had missed the beautiful stone buildings and the huge maple trees on Mesrop Mashtots Boulevard. I touched the walls, trying to bring back memories. In the springtime, the streets of Erevan were full of the sounds of birds, returning after winter. The birds were so loud that sometimes it was impossible even to talk. Everything looked familiar, but something had changed. Then I understood. Erevan had lost its spirit. The faces of the people had changed. It had once been a proud and prosperous European city where the inhabitants had high self-esteem. I wished that she could get back her charm and dignity, and that the people who lived in this city could be happy and proud again.

It was painful to see people in such poor conditions, difficult to accept. Maybe this is the price of independence and the new capitalistic economy. Now there is a deep gap between the rich and the poor. The people are 80 percent poor and 20 percent rich. There is no middle class.

My mother, Oktiabrina, takes this very seriously. She said she didn't see anything good. She felt that we were losing our nation. The new buildings were not for ordinary people, only for people with money. People with university degrees were begging for money. She thought it would be impossible to survive there. She thought it was better under communism because now people are only thinking about their pockets. My mother is an optimistic person, always trying to see the good. But in Armenia she saw that there was more bad than good.

Reflections

I was very fragile before. I was like a flower under the glass. Everything was good. Everyone took care of me. One of Souren's American friends asked him, "Why do you need a Russian princess?" I was raised on books, and books are not the real world. Now I see that the world is very wide. Before, my world was my country, my city, my street, my friends, my movies, my music, my books. I am stronger than I used to be. I am a different person. I have been influenced by my life here. My mother thinks I have become ruder and harder. She sees me as tired, not the same person I was before. But she also sees me as more independent.

You have to work hard in a capitalistic society. Because of competition, you need to be disciplined. You need strong elbows to fight your way up the ladder. It's the law of the wolf. Sometimes you lose your heart and soul. When I first saw homeless people, I was surprised and angry. You are an American, you know the language, and you are not an immigrant. Then I understood. Maybe one day something happened. Maybe they got a divorce or maybe they got sick. They lost their home and ended up on the street. They were not strong enough to move forward, to survive. I have a customer who was a writer, a very nice lady. She used to buy scarves. One day she told me that she was living in a shelter. Her teeth were in terrible condition. It can happen to anybody. Now when I see people on the streets, I wonder, "What got them here?"

One thing I have noticed is that here you are responsible for yourself. Many of my young co-workers live on their own without parents. They work hard all day and many work overtime. Then they go home to study. They work to pay their rent, insurance and bills. They don't even have time to read or go to museums. They go through sicknesses, dangerous things, drugs, wrong relationships, and nobody can stop them because their parents live far away. Maybe this is a good exercise to make them stronger, but sometimes they are making terrible mistakes and nobody is there to stop them. Armenian children live with their families until they get married and after that their parents still help them.

Armenian parents want to give everything to their children. They love and often spoil them. We can live badly, but our kids have to live better. Then when the children grow up, they switch roles and take care of their parents. There is a cycle between parent and child. We respect and pay attention to our old people. At work I see a lot of old, lonely people. Sometimes they spend all day at the store. Maybe their children live far away and they can't see them. I couldn't think of leaving my mom by herself. It would be a nightmare for me if someone else took care of her

This country has given me a lot.
I have cried a lot.
I have worked a lot.
This has become my country too.

Americans are paying a high price for their independence. I am telling you that with independence comes loneliness. It's difficult for Armenians to be lonely. It's like damnation. In America, people are very busy and always in a rush. I think they are missing out on a lot. Here it's a luxury to see people and communicate with them.

In Armenia, we would always meet over a cup of coffee and talk about our lives. This closeness is like therapy. We pay for a coffee and get therapy. It seems that every American has a psychotherapist. This is because they have no one to talk to. Everybody likes their privacy, but here it's pathological. We don't have a concept of privacy in Armenia. If something happens, everybody tries to help. It's about survival. There is a saying, "Don't have $100; have 100 friends." This proverb comes from the Soviet Union where most people didn't have any wealth. What they had instead was family and friends. You can't be depressed when you have people who care about you.

Duality in my Soul

I miss my country. I miss my young years. I miss being a teacher, I miss my students. I have been here for sixteen years. This country has given me a lot. I have cried a lot. I have worked a lot. This has become my country too. Before, I thought it would be easy to go back, but now it would be difficult. When I say I am going back, this is not sincere. Something is keeping me here. My work, the people, friends, this street—this is also my life.

From here I see that Armenia is poor and fragile and needs our help and support. The United States is a rich, strong, dominating stepmother compared to Armenia. We have a poor mother, but she is our country. There is an Armenian proverb that says, "At first we admire our parents, then we criticize them, and at the end we pity them." There is a duality in my soul. I am physically here, but my soul is still in Armenia, yet I cannot imagine starting my life over again. You cannot step twice in the same river.

My Dream

It's a beautiful sunny day at Zvartnots International Airport in Erevan, Armenia. Airplanes are lining up to land. Armenians from around the world continue coming back home to Armenia. The headlines in the newspapers say, "Unbelievable Economic Boom in Armenia." Everyone is living a prosperous and stable life, smiles and happiness all around. There is no crime and corruption. Wide and beautiful highways are taking people to the cities. The borders with our neighbors are opened. There is no crime and corruption. Biblical Ararat can relax. There is no more turmoil for this brave and loyal nation. The government of Turkey accepts the Armenian Genocide.

I recently read an article about the life of Pope John Paul II. In the article he spoke about the history of his country, Poland, which has a parallel history to ours. He could have been talking about Armenia. "I am the son of a nation who was condemned by his neighbors to death. My nation survived, not because they are physically strong, but because of their culture."

Nara at the beach in Los Angeles, 2000.

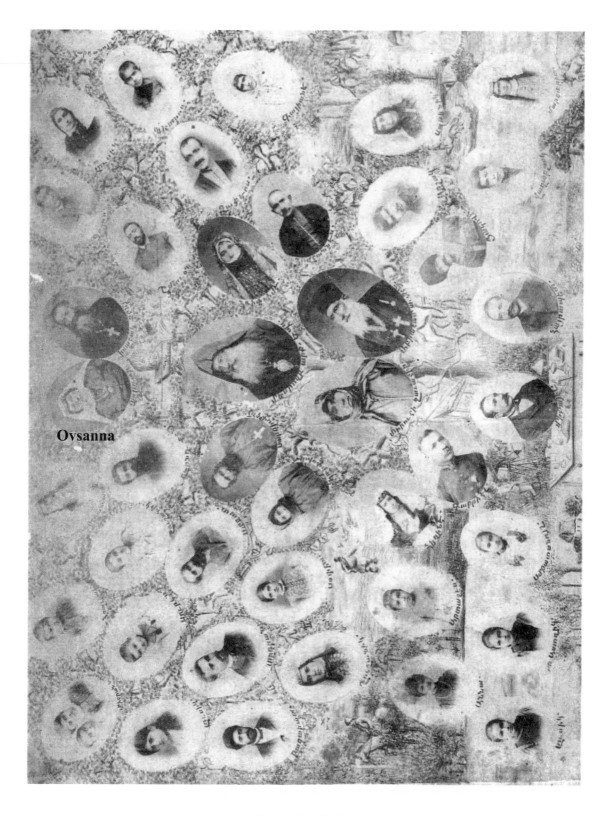

Ovsanna

Nara's Family Tree

Xidan's Story

Xidan Wang was born in Chongqing City, Sichuan Province, in southwest China on October 1, 1953, on Chinese National Day. This day marks the establishment of the People's Republic of China. She graduated from medical school in 1977, and at the age of twenty-seven started her career as a doctor in the Fifth People's Hospital of Chongqing City. While working at the hospital, as China was opening its doors to the world, she trained as a plastic surgeon and built a highly successful, full-service beauty spa business. In 1997, Xidan married an American businessman from Taiwan, and they moved to the United Stateson on July 4, 1998. Here is Xidan's story.

Xidan

My Family

When the Japanese invaded China, they came through Lianyun Harbor City of Jiangsu Province, which was where my mother's family had lived for nine generations. My mother, born in 1924, was the youngest of five children. Her family was extremely rich, and for a number of generations many of her family members held high positions in the Qing Dynasty. While I was growing up, my mother rarely mentioned her family, but according to my cousin, most of the businesses in the city were owned by just three families; one was my mother's. These businesses included banks; pawn shops; jewelry, clothing, grocery and fabric stores; as well as farmland outside the city. The three families married only each other, making them all cousins. In traditional China, people could only marry someone from their same social class. A rich man could never marry a poor woman, but he could take her as his mistress, and many did. My grandfather had many mistresses, but my grandmother would not allow him to bring them home.

Historical Note:

The Japanese occupation of China started in the early 1930s when Japan occupied Manchuria, but the war did not really start until 1937 in northern China and lasted eight years until August 1945. During the period that the Japanese occupied China, there were two political parties in the country: the Chinese Communist Party (CCP) and the Kuomintang (KMT or the Nationalist Party). The KMT, the party in power, was led by Chiang Kai-shek while Mao Zedong led the CCP.

When the Japanese invaded Lianyun Harbor, they took over the whole city, including my mother's house. Her family, along with the other two families,

The Japanese invasion of China brought together people of different political ideologies because everyone was affected.

was able to flee to the countryside, but when they returned, everything was gone. The Japanese did horrible things to the Chinese. They raped women, even pregnant women, and killed children. They had no respect for our culture. In schools, students were forced to learn Japanese instead of Chinese. They stole everything they could. They even took the special clothing and jade jewelry my mother's family had placed in their caskets to protect their bodies for the afterlife. There are no words to express the horrible things they did. It was a nightmare. The Japanese invasion of China brought together people of different political ideologies because everyone was affected. My two uncles and aunties joined the Chinese Communist Party (CCP). Like many others in China, they were ashamed that the Japanese had invaded China, and they felt that the Kuomintang (KMT) was too weak to fight against them. They were also attracted to the high ideals of the CCP, especially the desire to help poor people.

My father was born in 1924 in Xanxi Province, Xi'an City. His family owned land. Compared to most people, my father's family was rich, but not anywhere as rich as my mother's. When my father was two years old, his mother died of a round worm in her intestines. At that time in China, hygiene was very bad, and people didn't have access to routine medical care. There was no medicine to treat this disease, even for rich people, and the transportation was so bad that she couldn't get to the hospital in the city in time. In the end, she vomited the worm, suffocated and died. After many years, my grandfather remarried, and he and his wife had a baby boy.

In 1939, when my father was fifteen years old, he joined the underground movement of the CCP. My grandfather was so worried about his safety that he pressured my father to get married, hoping this would keep him at home. Even though my father was only a teenager, he followed his father's wishes and got married. Soon after, he and his wife had a baby boy. The problem was that my father didn't want to have a family; what he wanted was to fight for the nation. He believed that his country should come before his family. My grandfather threatened my father. He told him, "If you leave home to join the underground, I will never see you again." This didn't change my father's mind. When my father was seventeen, people from the underground movement in his city gave him a new name, Zheng, which means a sharp weapon, and helped him leave home. The underground moved my father from house to house until he reached Fudon University in Shanghai City, and once there, he spent his time studying math and

31

organizing students to fight against the KMT and support the ideas of Mao. My father never saw his father again, and he left not knowing that his wife was pregnant with his second child, a daughter. I didn't meet my sister until I was eight years old, and I never met my brother.

In 1946, my mother followed her sister to Shanghai, where their family owned a business, and enrolled in the Missionary Nursing School. People from the underground movement of the CCP recruited her, and like my father, she took on a revolutionary name. Her new name was Hui, which means bright like sunshine. In 1949, three months before the new government came to power, my parents joined with other students to participate in a special three-month training program in Nanjing, the previous capital of the Kuomintang Government, to prepare students to become officers in the new government. Deng Xiaoping, who later rose to a high position in the government along with many other high-level people from the military, trained the students in how to build the new country. The students were divided into three groups, and each was sent to a different region in China. My parents, along with 2,500 other students, were sent to the southwest part of China. Their group was called the People's Republic of China's Southwest Service Group.

On October 1, 1949, on the train from Nanjing to Changde City, the students listened to the radio as Chairman Mao announced in Tiananmen Square at the Gate of Heavenly Peace (a building in Tiananmen Square), "The Chinese people have stood up." According to my mother, everyone was crying like children, hugging each other, cheering, yelling and throwing their hats up in the air. Everyone had dreamed of this day, fought for this day, and hoped for this day. They felt they could devote their hearts and souls to their new country. Everyone felt proud, filled with the spirit of nationalism, and everyone pledged to be committed to the revolution forever. My mother told me that her new life began when she joined with the students to fight for the new China.

When the students arrived in Changde City, they began their long walk to Chongqing City of Sichuan Province. They walked about thirty miles each day for about two months, each carrying a backpack filled with seven kilograms of food and their personal belongings. Because my mom was a nurse, she often walked an additional ten miles a day. If she was at the front of the line and found out that someone was sick at the end of the line, she would have to run back to help them. The trip was full of danger. The students were not armed but a small group of the Liberation Army fought ahead of them because Sichuan Province was still in the hands of the KMT. The conditions were terrible. Many of the roads were nothing more than narrow dirt paths, and in some cases there were no paths at all. To protect themselves from insects and snakes, the students tied the bottom of each pant leg. Shoes were a big problem. Most of the students wore handmade shoes made from straw or cotton, and some students didn't wear any shoes at all. Often the entire soles of their feet would be covered with blisters.

Every night my mother would soak their feet *They had the "hot blood of patriotism."*

in hot water and pierce the blisters with a needle that she had put in the fire to sanitize. Despite all the hardships, each morning, no matter what, the students would begin their walk again. There was no way they could stop and rest, no matter how hard it was.

According to my mother, although they had no showers and no beds, and lived in bad conditions, no one complained. They had the "hot blood of patriotism." Their mission and sense of responsibility pushed them forward to help people. Whenever they stopped in towns, the students would sing patriotic songs to encourage the local people, and the local people would offer the students grain and other goods. Often my mother led the songs. Whenever I spoke about this with my mother, I could feel the excitement still in her voice.

Everyone felt that Mao Zedong was like a god. He had big ideals for China. He wanted to make all people equal, no rich or poor. My mother believed strongly in this goal. She never understood why some people were born poor and others rich. When my mother was a child, she would always play with the children of the poor people. She told me that she never felt lucky for being born rich. Mao also believed that men and women should be equal. During the older generations, women didn't work outside the home. They were dependent on their husbands, and if they weren't married, they were dependent on their parents. My mother hated these old traditions. All of this changed with the revolution because Mao believed in total equality between men and women. For me, gender equality is one of the most important accomplishments of the Communist Revolution, and it has continued to this day. I am very proud of that.

Once the group arrived in the southwest part of China, students left to work in small towns as managers. My parents were dropped off in Chongqing City, the capital of the KMT. My parents didn't know each other on the march. They didn't meet until they were working for the new government in Chongqing City. They married in 1952, and I was born a year later. A year after, my brother Xio Li was born. My Chinese name is Xidan Wang. In China, parents give their children, especially the first baby, names that symbolize their wishes, goals and hopes. When I was born, many Chinese children were given Russian names because China had a strong friendship with Russia. I am named after a famous Russian girl named Danya who was killed by the Germans in World War II when she was eighteen because she worked for the underground movement. In Russia, she is a heroine. I am also named for the color red because at that time in China, everything red was good, and I am named after the city Wuxi, which is close to my mother's hometown.

My father was first assigned to the General Labor Association, which was responsible for taking over the factories from the capitalist owners, and in 1953, when my father was twenty-nine, he became chief of the Ministry of Financial Affairs in the Southern District,

> *"We gave you the biological body, but you are not our private property. You belong to this country."*

Chongqing City. My mother was assigned to the Propaganda Department in City Hall, which was responsible for a broad range of programs, including primary education, health, cultural activities and public opinion. One of the main goals of the new government was to eliminate illiteracy in China. Mao wanted all people to be educated. My mother's job was to go to factories to teach people to read. Sometimes she didn't come home at night because the factories were too far and there was no convenient transportation. My mother and father were passionate about their work and totally committed to building the new country. They taught us that the good of the country always comes first. There was no individualism. Even talking about individualism was shameful. My parents always told us, "We gave you the biological body, but you are not our private property. You belong to this country." My sense of nationalism and pride in my country come from my family. My parents taught us that for life to make sense, you must have a bigger goal and a higher purpose. We call that the big "I."

> *My parents taught us that for life to make sense, you must have a bigger goal and a higher purpose. We call that the big "I."*

During this time, everyone had a strong feeling of sacrifice. Government workers worked more than fourteen hours a day, six days a week. Saturday was the only day married couples could be together. Many government workers sent their children to live with nannies because they didn't have time to be with them. It was easy to find nannies; labor was cheap. After my brother was born, each of us had our own nanny, and then when I was three and my brother was two, we moved to the same nanny's home. We called her "Nanny Momma." My parents dropped by during the weekends to take us out for meals, but we always went back to the nanny's home to sleep. Before I was eight I didn't understand why I had two mothers and why one mother gave money to the other. When I was eight years old and more independent, my brother and I went back to live with my parents, but I saw my Nanny Momma many times while I was growing up. She didn't have children. I was like her daughter. I loved her very much.

My Early Life

My family lived in a one-room government apartment with no kitchen or bathroom. Unmarried people lived in their offices. We had to keep our clothes in suitcases because there were no closets. Families were not allowed to cook at home. We all ate together in a canteen, where people also got their bottled water. At that time, China was a third-world country. Water was not safe to drink, so each family brought their thermos to the canteen. There was one public bathroom and one public shower with twenty or thirty stalls that everyone shared. There were no toilets, only one long hole in the ground. Each morning there was a long line of people waiting to use the toilet or to wash.

Everyone in the new government wanted to be considered "red," and if you grew up in a rich family, you had "black" blood.

Life for my parents was very different from how they had grown up, especially for my mother, who had grown up very rich and spoiled and was used to people serving her. At this time, she was ashamed of her background, and considered her childhood to be a "dirty spot" on her life.

Everyone in the new government wanted to be considered "red," and if you grew up in a rich family, you had "black" blood. My parents didn't want anyone to know that they had grown up in a rich family, so they never talked about their families, and we didn't have any family pictures in our apartment. I didn't learn anything about my family until I was a teenager during the Cultural Revolution.

My Education

In the new government, education was free for boys and girls, and by law every child had to go to school. If families wanted their children to work instead, government workers would go to their home and demand that they send their children to school. I started elementary school when I was six years old. The curriculum included Chinese, history, math, politics, and the arts, and then in middle school all students learned Russian as their second language. I also took free dancing and gymnastics classes at the community center in my city.

When I started elementary school, I applied to become a member of the Red Collar Group, which included children seven to sixteen years old. The red collar symbolized the desire to become a part of the new movement, and almost all the students joined. The Youth Communist Group, which was for students sixteen to twenty years old, was much more difficult to join, and only about half the students were accepted. To join, you had to be an honor student, have a special talent like dancing or singing, agree with Mao's ideas and do good actions, like helping people. I joined this group during my first year in medical school. After this, you could become a Communist Party member, which I never did. For one thing, I couldn't join because of my family's bad background, but the main reason I didn't join was that the Cultural Revolution destroyed my generation's belief in communism.

My Life during the Cultural Revolution

During the Cultural Revolution, the whole country stopped. The government stopped working. The students stopped studying. I was thirteen years old when the Cultural Revolution started and had been in school for a total of six years.

Every day we took *Mao's Little Red Book* everywhere and reflected on our thoughts and actions. We wore army clothing with red armbands and a pin with Mao's picture on it. We all had a picture of Mao hanging on our walls. Here you have a picture of Jesus Christ, but at that time in China we had a picture of Mao.

Every morning, I woke up to the sounds of a loudspeaker playing music outside our home. When the loudspeaker played, we stopped what we were doing, took out *Mao's Little Red Book* we kept in our pocket, held the book to our heart, and began to dance and sing: "Dear Chairman Mao, you are the red sun in our hearts. Your thoughts are our lifeline. We will smash whoever opposes Chairman Mao. People all over the world love our great leader, Chairman Mao." This was like a prayer. My father was embarrassed to dance, but because he wanted to show his loyalty to the government, he practiced in our house so he could join the dancing. If you didn't dance, people might think you were disloyal.

The Red Guard divided people into three categories: red, black and gray. People in the red category came from families of workers, peasants, revolutionary officials, revolutionary officers and revolutionary martyrs. People in the black category, like my parents, came from families of landlords, rich peasants, antirevolutionaries, bad elements (like petty criminals), and rightists. People in the gray category came from ambiguous families, such as shop assistants and clerks. The Red Guard checked your family background going back three generations. Despite the fact that my parents had been rich landowners, I was put into the gray category because they had helped to build the new country.

Because of my parents' "bad background," my brother and I couldn't join the Red Guard, which made life terrible for us. The Red Guard stoned us and called us "sons of bitches." I was always fighting them to protect my brother. I still have a scar on my face from when the Red Guard threw stones at me. I never car-

Xidan and her mother in 2004 standing in front of the building they lived in during the Cultural Revolution.

ried my house key because the Red Guard would take the key to rob my house, so every time we went back home I had to climb through a window. I blamed my parents for marrying each other and having kids.

My mother loved to read and had a very good collection of international literature, including books by American, Russian and French authors. One day the Red Guard burned all my mother's books and pictures. When I got home, she was sitting in a chair looking very sad. She hadn't been able to stop them. She could only watch. I was not sympathetic because I had done the same thing to other people. My mother never felt sad for the loss of her other belongings, but she always felt sad about the loss of these books. After the end of the Cultural Revolution, my mother bought these same books again, and today they're famous in China.

During the first year of the Cultural Revolution, my parents were sent to a labor camp at least three times. They came home for one night every two or three weeks. Each day they studied *Mao's Little Red Book*, reflecting on what they had ever thought, how they had ever behaved, and whether their actions had been bad. They tried to figure out the root of these bad thoughts and to see if there was any connection to the thoughts of Liu Shaoqi and Deng Xiaoping. If the Red Guard believed that my parents' thoughts were correct, they would be released,

During that time, I stopped calling them Father and Mother and just called them antirevolutionaries. Every family in China was destroyed by the Cultural Revolution.

but if the Red Guard thought there were problems, they would have to stay.

One day my father came home alone and told us that our mother might not be able to come back. Because she had left her parents' home after she was twenty-two years old and was considered independent, she was not categorized as a child of landlords but as a landlord, which was more serious. My mother continued to write and reflect about how she had exploited the peasants, although she never had. Sometimes the Red Guard paraded my parents on the streets of my city and let people throw eggs and cabbage at them. I threw eggs harder than anyone else to prove that I was a revolutionary. Since my brother and I were little, we had no other way to prove that we were red except by criticizing our parents harder than anyone else.

We had almost no conversation with our parents. If we needed to talk to them, we gave them orders. When my father couldn't bear it anymore, he brought us to him and pleaded that he and my mother were not antirevolutionaries. My brother cried. I kicked him and told him to stop crying, that our parents were liars who were trying to deceive us with their tears. I was loyal to Mao, not to my family. In traditional China, it was very important to respect your parents and call them Father and Mother. During that time, I stopped calling them Father and Mother and just called them antirevolutionaries. Every family in China was destroyed by the Cultural Revolution.

My family had many, many sad stories. My brother's father-in-law, who was also one of my father's best friends, committed suicide by jumping into the Yangtze River. My mother was afraid that my father might also commit suicide, so she asked me to follow him wherever he went. I refused. At that time I thought about getting a gun to kill my father because he was an antirevolutionary. This thought tortured me for many years. I also thought about killing myself, but I didn't know how to commit suicide because I was only thirteen.

My mom's oldest sister had married a man who had worked for the KMT. After the Revolution in 1949, he and my aunt stayed in China. My aunt became a principal of a famous girls' school in Shanghai, and her husband held a high position in the new government. During the Cultural Revolution, the students called him a spy and took him off to jail. My aunt was put on stage and tortured everyday by her students. One day when she couldn't stand it anymore, she hanged herself in her home. My mom's other sister was the head of a large factory, and her husband held a high position in Shanghai City Hall. The students beat them with a leather belt every day, claiming that they were part of the bourgeoise. He jumped from a sixth-floor window and died. My aunt survived. My mom's oldest brother, who had a high position in An Wui City, died in jail. My mom's other brother was okay because he was not in such a high position. My father's younger brother was sent to jail where he died for criticizing Vice Chairman Lin Biao.

In 1970, as the Cultural Revolution came to an end, many people went back to their old jobs. My father went back to work for the government in a lower position than he held before, and in 1973 he returned to his old position as chief of the Bureau of Financial Affairs for the Southern Region. Later, my mother returned to her job also. The older generation never complained about what happened to them. They believed that because they had come from a black background, they deserved this treatment to prove that they were not antirevolutionaries. They thought that suffering made them better communists. To this day, people in China still have not talked about what happened during the Cultural Revolution.

Working with Farmers in the Countryside

By the summer of 1968 when I was fifteen years old, Chairman Mao asked students to go to the mountains or the countryside to work at the bottom of the society and receive re-education from the farmers. The regulation said that only students over sixteen could go to the countryside, but I was tough and I wanted to prove that I was a revolutionary so I registered myself. My school rewarded me for doing this because even though my parents were against it, I went anyway. My parents thought it was dangerous, but they still had to present a positive attitude about my participation.

As bus after bus left for the countryside, we sang songs and cheered. All the students felt an obligation to help the people. We all felt the same "hot blood of patriotism" that my parents felt when they walked from Changde City to Chongqing in 1949 to help build the new China. When the bus left, my father cried.

Once we arrived in the countryside, we were sent to different areas. I went to Linshui County, Da Xian District in Sichuan Province, which was a mountain area about four hours by bus from Chongqing. The conditions in the village were very poor. The farmers got their water from a local well and used kerosene lamps for light. They slept on straw beds with straw blankets. Some very poor families had only one pair of pants, which meant that the person who went to work wore the pants. The other people covered themselves with straw.

*Historical Note:
In 1968, six million students went to the countryside to work for the "collective welfare" of the country, and to learn about poverty and hardship from the farmers.*

When we arrived at the farm, every student received a quota of food for six months and a small piece of land to plant our own vegetables. It took about six months before the vegetables we had planted were ready to eat. I didn't know how to cook, so I gave my quota of food to the farmer's family in exchange for eating meals with them. The farmers were happy to do this because the food we got was much better than what the farmers ate.

Each morning I woke up before sunrise and walked one hour to the farm where I spent my day with forty or fifty people planting vegetables like corn, beans, sweet potatoes and rice. At 10 a.m. I walked back to my shed, and at 3 in the afternoon, I would walk back again to continue planting until 8 at night. I didn't know how to farm so I got horrible blisters on my hands. My home was a storage shed. Often at night I would hear rats running around the room, and sometimes in the morning I would awake to find a dead rat in my water bucket.

Every Saturday on Market Day, we met with our friends from the nearby farms and shared our experiences. Often we would cry together. In the beginning the farmers welcomed the students. But some of the students were not good workers. Some stole chickens and vegetables from the farmers. On the other hand, there were some bad farmers. There were farmers who raped the girls. Many of my classmates felt abandoned and betrayed by the government, and their enthusiasm was crushed. In China, we have a saying: "So dark you could not see the sky or the sun." This is how many of the students felt.

I had a good relationship with the farmers, and they all called me "comrade," which was a sign of deep respect. In Chinese this means "same big ideal," and it was unusual to refer to a child this way. But life in the countryside was hard. During the week there was no one I could talk to. Psychologically I suffered a lot, and after one month when I couldn't bear to live this hard life, I thought about killing myself. I considered slicing my throat, but thought it would be too painful. I thought about hanging myself, but there were too many ugly stories in traditional China about people who transformed into evil ghosts after hanging themselves. Then I thought about using drugs, but I couldn't find any, and I didn't know what kind of drugs to take or how many doses I needed. So in the end I decided to starve myself to death. One day when I didn't go to work or to eat, the farmer came looking for me. I told him I wanted to die. He asked me if he had done anything wrong. He was a good man. He treated me like his daughter.

One Saturday on Market Day, I saw someone from the military who was recruiting people to perform for soldiers. When I was little, I was fond of gymnastics and dancing, so I decided to audition for them, and when they asked me to join, I accepted. I knew that the military would provide me with everything I needed, so when I left, I gave away everything to the farmers: my clocks, moon guitar, clothes, and blanket. The farmers felt bad about my leaving, thinking that they had done something wrong. They were very simple and warm people. When I was in medical school, I went back to visit them many times and invited them to visit me in the city. I was like my mom. I got along with all kinds of people.

I was placed in the Art and Literature Group of the Railroad Soldiers as a member of the performance troupe of the artistic army, which was a special branch of the People's Liberation Army (PLA). The job of the Railroad Army was to build a railroad from Sichuan to Shanxi. The job of the performance troupe was not only to perform for soldiers but also to compete with other artistic armies and local performance groups. I danced and played the *pipa*, a traditional Chinese musical instrument that you hold on your lap.

Becoming a "Barefoot Doctor"

In 1971, five years after the start of the Cultural Revolution, the universities reopened. The work of the artistic army was also completed, and the government offered everyone in my group a job in the city. I refused. My goal was to go to the university and live the life of an educated person; and I knew that in order to be accepted into the university, I needed to build my experience and create a "good history."

I thought if I returned to the countryside, I could accomplish this, so when I finished my two-year service in the artistic army, I returned to the countryside, but this time to become a "barefoot doctor." Before the Cultural Revolution, most farmers didn't have any medical help. If someone was sick, they would have to travel as far as fifty miles to get help. During the Cultural Revolution, students traveled with doctors to the countryside to help the farmers and learn traditional medicine, like herbs and acupuncture. These students were called "barefoot doctors." I had no medical knowledge. I just followed the doctors from house to house, sometimes walking as many as twenty-five miles a day, carrying a medicine box and learning everything I could about traditional medicine. I saw sick people healed by acupuncture. No pills, no surgery, just a little needle. Seeing that, I wanted to go to medical school to do something to help people. I also wanted to become a doctor because that was my mother's dream for me.

First, I had to pass the entrance exam to the university. The university entrance exam was simple. It had to be. Schools had been shut down for several years. Nobody had studied. My father received permission to come to the countryside to tutor me for the exam. At this time, my father was still "standing on the sidelines," meaning he had not yet returned to his high position in the government, and he was able to convince his boss that he needed to go to the countryside to receive additional re-education. My father enjoyed this time very much. He was very comfortable around farmers because until he left his city to join the underground movement when he was seventeen years old, he had lived on a farm and had become friendly with the farmers.

The exam covered three subjects: Chinese composition, math, and politics, which meant studying and commenting on Mao's thoughts. I passed the examination in July of 1973, but my top choice for a university rejected me because my family background was "gray." Fortunately, my father was "liberated" around

> *Even though there were vaccines against common diseases for children, many children died because villagers could not get them.*

this time, which erased my family's bad record, and I was accepted at another college, the North Sichuan Medical College in Nanchong, Sichuan Province.

Starting Medical School

In September of 1973, I began the next phase of my life, this time as a medical student. Even though I had only spent six years in school, it felt natural to be there because I always loved to read and study. The students were all different ages. I was nineteen years old, and the head of my class was almost fifty.

During my fourth and last year of medical school, I was sent to the county hospital in Langzhong County, the highest-level hospital for the villagers, and rotated through all the departments, like internal medicine, surgery, neurology, gynecology and infectious diseases, which interested me the most. I saw many diseases that I had only learned about in textbooks, including parasitic diseases caused by round worm, which is how my grandmother died, as well as hook worm, hydrophobia, elephant skin, diphtheria, and hemorrhagic fever. Even though there were vaccines against common diseases for children, many children died because villagers could not get them.

I was sent to work in a clinic in the countryside. Conditions were terrible. The clinic didn't even have sterilization equipment; they sterilized their knives and needles by putting them into a pot of boiling water. Each clinic served an area of thirty square miles with just one doctor, one nurse and the medical students. I remember one night a man came running up to the clinic crying for help. He said that his wife was in labor and that the baby was in the wrong birthing position. The doctor, nurse and I walked for fourteen miles in a rain storm to get to their home, falling many times because the roads were so muddy. We arrived at 4 a.m. shortly after the baby had been born. The scene was very bloody. The woman had been in so much pain that she had cut open her belly with a kitchen knife to take out the baby, but the mother and baby survived. I held a torch to help the doctor and nurse see because there was no electricity in the house. The mother never even got an infection. She was lucky. Many babies died during childbirth at this time. Villagers are really tough. They can survive all kinds of situations.

Opening an Infectious Disease Department

In 1977, I became a doctor, and three years later I returned to Chongqing City to work at the Number Five People's Hospital, an affiliated hospital of the Chongqing Medical University. When I started working at the hospital, there was no infectious disease department. Patients with infectious diseases were put into the internal medicine department with other patients, increasing the opportunity for infection. I was determined to do something to change this. I worked with other doctors and nurses to turn an abandoned area in the hospital into an infectious disease department. I had six doctors and twelve nurses working for me.

At twenty-eight, I had become the youngest chief of a department in Chongqing City. I loved my work. I loved helping people. But I often felt helpless. There were no treatments or medicines for some of the diseases I saw. There was no way to make people better. Every day I faced these sad faces and couldn't do anything about it. As a doctor, if you can't solve people's problems, you feel very sad.

Starting My Cosmetology Business

Before the economic reforms in China, women looked like they were in the army. No one had any style. They wore two colors, green and gray. They all had short, straight hair. They couldn't wear leather shoes or high heels, only simple tennis shoes. They couldn't wear any makeup or jewelry, and they all wore pants. People who wore colorful clothes were called "witches" or "metamorphic spirits." After the opening of China, everybody wanted to be beautiful. Everybody wanted to change their faces, bodies, eyes and noses. The whole country was changing.

As the economy flourished during the early 1990s and people had money to spend, more spas opened up. Encouraged by my friends, I decided to take the risk and open up my own. I felt I had the skills to do this. I had learned anatomy and plastic surgery in medical school, and when I was a performer in the army, I had learned about make-up, fashion and color. I had also learned how to run a business from running my department in the hospital. Though many businesses were opening up in China, there were no business programs in colleges or universities, like those in the United States. People relied on their prior experience and knowledge to run their businesses.

I created a full-service beauty salon in the center of my city where women could come to one place for everything they needed: facials, massage, make-up, manicures, hairstyling, exercise and even surgery. I also set up a school to train students in advanced facials and massage using traditional Chinese approaches like acupuncture. I supervised a staff of twenty-four, including two doctors, five nurses and a manager for each department. Everyone who

After the opening of China, everybody wanted to be beautiful. Everybody wanted to change their faces, bodies, eyes and noses.

Historical Note:
In 1978, the government put into effect a number of economic reforms, and by 1986, the Chinese economy was flourishing. These reforms, started by Deng Xiaoping, focused on agriculture, industry, science and technology, and the military. They were called "socialism with Chinese characteristics." The purpose was to open China to the world, to start its export-oriented economy, and to preserve the CCP's party-state dominance in politics and society at the same time. People started to run their own businesses.

touched a person's body had to be at least a nurse. My spa was very successful. In my city, women were beautiful and always wanted to be more beautiful. If my customers only had enough money to eat lunch or have a facial, they would choose a facial.

Often my customers didn't know how to improve their looks. Some would bring a picture of a famous movie star to use as their model. One day a woman came in who wanted her nose to look like Audrey Hepburn's. The problem was that this woman had a big face, small eyes and a flat nose. In China, women want to look like Western women with whiter skin, big blue eyes, a high nose, small face and big breasts. In the United States, women go to tanning stores to make their skin darker, and they have surgery to make their noses smaller and lower. Everyone wants what they don't have. All they really want is change.

Some women wanted surgery because their boyfriends thought that their eyes were too small or their nose was too low or their skin was not good. I told them that I wouldn't do surgery for their boyfriends. I told them, "You look good; you just don't know how to make yourself better." I always pushed my customers to have more confidence and to become more independent, and I was always honest with them. I turned down a lot of customers. Some people would say, "This doctor is funny; I offer her money and she refuses."

In 1994, the government established a national organization based in Beijing to develop national

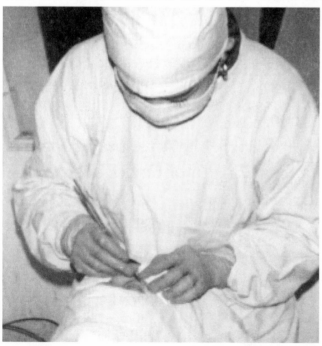

Xidan operating on a patient in her spa, 1992.

44

Xidan at a medical conference in Bejing, 1995.

standards to regulate these spas. I became vice president of the Chongqing branch and was on the committee that established national standards for surgery and cosmetology. I also wrote textbooks to train students to pass the cosmetology license exam, helped draft questions for the exam, and wrote several chapters for a comprehensive book about plastic surgery and cosmetology. Every year I delivered a paper on a different aspect of cosmetology, such as the use of acupressure in body massage, and new ways to do eye surgery. I was invited to different cities to perform cosmetic surgery. Even though many beauty salons had special rooms to do plastic surgery, most did not have doctors to perform the surgery.

> *I was "walking up hill," which means that I was getting better and better, reaching the top of the mountain.*

By Chinese standards, I was very successful. I was "walking up hill," which means that I was getting better and better, reaching the top of the mountain. I always wanted to be at the top. When I worked at the hospital, I wanted my skills to get better and better. This was the same in my business. I always think—how can I make things better, including myself? I always challenge myself. This is my personality.

My First Marriage

When I was twenty-five, my family decided that it was time for me to get married. They were worried that people would gossip. I was beautiful and healthy. Why did I reject marriage? For my parents' generation, getting married was a

> *I was fighting
> the old traditions
> about the role of women,
> but I had no choice.
> I had to consider the wishes of
> my parents*

stage in everyone's life, a task everyone had to fulfill. Not marrying would bring shame to my family. But I didn't want to get married. I wanted to live my own life, and for me, marriage meant losing myself to my family, husband and kids. I was fighting the old traditions about the role of women, but I had no choice. I had to consider the wishes of my parents.

I also knew that if I got married, I would have to have sex. I grew up thinking that sex was dirty, something men wanted and needed, but not women. Sex was only about carrying on the family. We didn't have any sex education programs as we do now, so no one knew anything about their bodies. During the Cultural Revolution, even talking about love or romance was considered capitalistic or bourgeois. The truth is that my deepest dream was to find a man who could be my soul mate. My idea of love came from my mother's collection of Western novels I read while I was growing up. These stories never included sex but viewed love as a spiritual connection.

Couples had to be introduced, usually by parents or friends, and one of the most important considerations was the political background of the families. In order to get married, a couple needed approval from their work bureau. The funniest part was that in their application, the couple would write that they were getting married for the sake of the revolution or to help build the new country. At that time there were no divorces in China. Now more people get married for the sake of love, and there is a 50-percent divorce rate.

In 1978, my family introduced me to Mr. Yang, who worked at the Chinese Research Institute of Science and Technology Information in Chongqing City. We exchanged information about our families, our college experiences and our hobbies. He was fond of art, and he played the trumpet. I thought we had some things in common. Three months later, we saw each other again. Most of the time, I was the one who talked. He was shy and introverted.

I told him that my first principle for a relationship was that he could not interfere with my career. I told him that before we even began to talk about marriage, we should spend the next two or three years encouraging each other in our careers, even competing with each other. This was different from most people in a relationship who talked about their future married life, how to save money, or where to live if they were assigned to different work places. To me these things were so vulgar and boring.

The second time we met, Mr. Yang tried to touch me. I didn't think that we were close enough for this and concluded that he was no different from other men. I told him I wanted to end the relationship and focus on my work. Mr. Yang talked with my parents about this, and as a result my father wrote me a fourteen-page letter about Mr. Yang's educational achievements and other advantages. My parents didn't understand me. In Chinese culture, children never discuss their insides with their parents.

After reading the letter from my father, I took a short trip to Xi'an City to give me time to think, and when I returned, there was a letter from Mr. Yang showing his sadness. I asked him to come see me so I could explain why I wanted to end our relationship. When I saw him, I felt so sad. He had dropped thirty pounds. Then I starting thinking that maybe everyone was right and I should get married. After all, he wasn't a bad person and he was sincere about getting married. The other reason I married him was that I never wanted to hurt my parents again. During the Cultural Revolution I had thought of stealing ammunition to kill my father, and even though I didn't do that, I felt very guilty about ever having had these thoughts.

Mr. Yang and I became engaged in 1979 and married in June of 1980. The day I got married, I didn't feel anything. I just followed my culture. During our three-day honeymoon (the government only allowed couples to have three days), I got pregnant. I had never thought about having children. I didn't want to be a woman who didn't have her own career or her own self, who waited on her husband and children. I am not a traditional Chinese woman. I have always followed my own mind. At that moment I felt I had no future.

> *Historical Note:*
> *The one-child policy was announced in January 1979 and executed in the early 1980s to control the population in China, which at that time was 1.1-billion people. Under this policy, couples need permission from their work units to have a child. The policy also gives mothers who work for the government one year of maternity leave with full salary.*

When I was close to my due date, my husband's parents asked me to come to their home in Chengdu City so they could take care of me. In China, grandparents always help after babies are born, and when there are no grandparents, couples hire a professional to take care of the mother and baby. My baby was born on April 30, 1981. I named him Hong Bin, wishing him ambition and great achievements. Women are given sixty days of paid postpartum rest. During this time, new mothers can't take a shower or comb and wash their hair. They have to wear a hat to cover their head and socks to keep their feet warm. They can only drink hot water and eat special foods. The windows have to be closed, even in summer. They are supposed to lie in bed and be served. They are not even allowed to read. They can only eat, sleep and feed the baby. These sixty days felt like prison. Whenever my in-laws left home, I would sneak out to look at books, and when I heard them coming back, I would hide the books. My mother-in-law, who was a gynecologist, knew about this and told me that reading would be bad for my eyes. This is so different from America. I have customers who go home immediately after delivery with no one to help them. This could cause damage to the woman's health.

After this childbirth period, I felt relieved because I could go back to work, and to my life. When I returned to work in Chongqing, my in-laws kept the baby with them. Six months after my son was born, the "one child" policy was put into effect, and I decided to use the last six months of allowed maternity leave to stay home with my son. I was worried that he would be spoiled by his grandparents, who valued boys more than girls. I didn't want him to be weak.

In China, even though it was against the law for men to hit women, the culture allowed it.

I brought the baby back to Chongqing City where, with my husband, we lived in my parents' home. Eventually, we moved into a room in the dormitory at my husband's research institute. Living conditions were much better for us than they were for my parents when they went to work for the new government. There still were no flushing toilets, but rather than one long hole in the ground, we had many holes, and they were separated by doors. Instead of one public shower, there were two, one for men and one for women, and in the room there were individual stalls. Some things hadn't changed. We still ate together in the canteen, and since water was not yet safe to drink, we filled up our thermos with clean water at the canteen.

When Hong Bin was one year old, I began to teach him how to count. Children, of course, resist this instruction. They cry and have irrational responses. My husband thought that the baby was too young to learn these things. We fought all the time. When my son was about sixteen months old, I decided to teach him how to read clocks. One afternoon I woke him from his nap to read clocks with him. My husband got so angry that he grabbed whatever he could to hit me. I could not tolerate that. I felt humiliated. I put my son on the floor and left the house. In China, even though it was against the law for men to hit women, the culture allowed it. Women never complained or sued the men. They accepted the abuse and never talked about it. They were too ashamed.

After my husband put my son to sleep, he came out looking for me, but I was hiding so he couldn't find me. While he was outside, I climbed through the window, took my clothes and left. I didn't know where to go. I couldn't go to my parents' home because I knew they would blame me. The only place I could think of was my Nanny Momma's home. My husband asked his parents to come to Chongqing to ask me to forgive him. They guaranteed that he wouldn't make the mistake of hitting me again, and they urged me to come home for the sake of the baby.

The seeds of divorce had been planted since the start of our married life.

There were always paradoxes. During the ten years we were married, we fought about our child's education, my work and our sex life. I was very busy building my infectious disease department. His work became stagnant, and the gap between us increased. When my child was a year old, I got pregnant again, but due to the one-child policy, I had to have an abortion. My husband wanted to have sex all the time, but I was very tired after work and I didn't want to get pregnant again. Many times he forced me. In China there were no laws against husbands raping their wives, like you have here.

The divorce happened suddenly. I needed to purchase a train ticket to attend a medical conference in southern China, but tickets were hard to come by at that time. One of my patients had an uncle who worked at the train station who was able to help. After I bought my ticket, my patient and I left the station together. In China at that time it was not acceptable for a woman to walk in public with a man who was not her husband. People would gossip. This was my culture. My husband saw us. When I got home, he became very angry and accused me of having an affair. Then he beat me up and raped me. There was nothing I could say or do to stop him. I knew I had to file for divorce.

My son stayed with his father, and I moved into a room at the hospital. I had many night shifts at the hospital so I was unable to take care of him during the week, but I saw my son every weekend. Still he was very sad. It was unusual for people to get divorced at this time, and my son didn't want anyone to know about it. He had a hard time.

After three months, I sued for divorce. At first, my husband refused to sign the divorce papers and mobilized everyone he could to stop me. He didn't think his behavior was wrong. This is because traditionally sex is a husband's right, and a woman can never say "no." In the past fifteen years, Chinese women have gained more equal rights in terms of work and family, but in terms of their sexual lives, it has remained mostly traditional.

I was fortunate to have a female judge because in China, many judges are men and influenced by traditional thoughts about marriage and divorce. The judge asked me why I had tolerated the abuse for so many years. I told her that violent sex and rape were not uncommon, but most people didn't speak out because they were too ashamed. The judge granted me a divorce and told me I was a hero for coming forward.

Life after My Divorce.

When my first marriage ended in 1991, I devoted almost all my time and energy to my work. I also started dancing again, which is how I met Mr. Ma, who was married at the time. Because of my social status, I was not allowed to have any scandal, and at that time people thought that dancing would cause family and social problems. But I have always done what I wanted to do, and soon Mr. Ma and I became dance partners. In order to avoid a scandal, I asked him to bring his wife to our practices. He never did. He had secretly divorced her.

Mr. Ma wanted us to compete as a couple. He told me that in order to win, we would need to nurture spontaneous actions, and to reach this level we would need to be lovers. Mr. Ma was more worldly and romantic than other men. He called me "darling" or "honey" and would open the door for me. He also taught me how to enjoy sex and made me realize that sex was a basic desire for women. We fell in love, and I moved in with him. Public opinion from my hospital, political party and parents was against this, but I didn't care. We had a love that combined mind and body, and I have never been a traditional Chinese woman. In fact, many of my friends have told me that I fit into Western culture better than Chinese culture.

Mr. Ma was really good at winning over my employees' hearts, and they all wanted to do massage for him. Some of my customers found his behavior suspicious with one of the girls who worked for me, but in the beginning I didn't believe them. Then one day I confronted Mr. Ma and he admitted that he had slept with that girl. I didn't say anything. I went home, packed my things and moved back to my parents' home. He was not loyal to me or responsible to this girl, who was only eighteen years old and had come from the countryside to the city to work. After this separation, I was in deep sorrow. This was the first time I knew what it felt like to be in love.

After my experience with Mr. Ma, I devoted myself completely to my work. Chinese men annoyed me. I thought there were only two kinds. The first was like my first husband, who was traditional. He was responsible to his family, but he treated me like a piece of property. The second kind was like Mr. Ma, who could not be responsible to his wife or family. He was a playboy, charming, handsome but not loyal.

Married Again

My family put a lot of pressure on me to get married again. At that time, single women did not live alone. Things have changed. Today women can live alone. They earn their own money and have the independence to determine their destiny. Because of the one-child policy, women spend less time taking care of their family and more time building their careers. But some things haven't changed. If the woman has a higher position or makes more money, the man appears weak, and Chinese women do not like weak men.

I met my future husband, Mr. Lin, in 1996 at an exhibition for new beauty products. Mr. Lin was an American citizen from Taiwan who had gone to China to find investment opportunities. I wasn't in love with him, but I trusted him and thought he would be different from Chinese men. I thought he would be more like the men I read about in Western novels who respected their wives. I also wanted to end the pressure I was getting from my family to get married, so a year or so after we met, we got married. My first wedding had been very simple. We had about fifteen family members and close friends, and served candy, cake and tea. My second wedding was totally different. China was changing. People had more money and they were spending it like crazy. Everything was very excessive. We invited 500 people and held the wedding in a big hotel. I hired a television host and ballroom dancers to perform.

Chongqing: Xidan's mother and father with Xidan's nephew on the left and her son, Hong Bin, on the right, 1984.

Coming to the United States

Even though we were married, I had no intention of ever moving to the United States to live with my husband. I had no reason to leave. My business was "like a flower in bloom." I thought we would live in different places. This is common in China. Many married couples live apart because they work in different places. After a few years of marriage, the couple can apply to live in the same place, but during the first years they live apart. But my husband always complained. He said this was not a marriage. He pushed and pushed me to come. I told him that I had a lot to lose by coming here, but he told me not to worry, that he would help me start a new business. I didn't ask any questions. I didn't ask for details. I trusted him. One and one-half years after we married, I gave up everything and moved here.

> *Even though we were married, I had no intention of ever moving to the United States to live with my husband.*

My family and about forty friends came to the airport in Chongqing to send me off. My mother, brother and son were sad, but my friends were happy and envious. They thought I was going to heaven. They thought that I was about to fall into a money hole. There was a general

I couldn't have a conversation with anyone because I didn't know the language. All I could do was smile.

belief that since the United States was the most developed country in the world, there would be more opportunities to be successful. I was more worried than happy. I didn't know what was waiting for me. I had no idea what America would be like. But I thought I would be able to find success. In reality, life here is very difficult. It's been much harder for me than I ever imagined.

I arrived in the United States on July 4, 1998, at 6 p.m. The airport in Los Angeles was big and crowded, not at all like the airports in China at that time. My first thought was that the United States was a special, big country. My husband's friend picked us up at the airport. When I

Xidan and her mother with the city of Chongqing in the background, 2004.

arrived at my new home in Gardena, I was so shocked that I almost passed out. The house was small and simple. It had an old sofa that my husband's friend had given him and a small television set. I couldn't believe that this was America. In China, I lived in a high-rise apartment with three large bedrooms. I had a large television set and a modern music system. Chongqing was a big, modern city with many tall buildings, thriving businesses, restaurants, stores and people on the street. Life was exciting and fast.

I had no idea how to start my new life in this strange country. There were no Chinese people living in the town and very few people on the streets. When I went outside the house, I couldn't have a conversation with anyone because I didn't know the

Historical Note:
Chongqing City is the most populous city in the world. It is also the fastest growing urban center in the world with one-half million people arriving every year hoping to find better opportunities. As of 2006, there were over 31.5 million people living there.

language. All I could do was smile. In China, I had learned Latin for my medical training and Russian in middle school, but I only knew a little English. Chinese people who come here say that if you don't have language, it's like living in a prison. I agree. For the first few months I spent every single day waiting for my husband to come home from work to drive me to adult school to learn English. I never went anywhere without my husband. I had no friends. No money. No language. When I watched television, I couldn't understand anything. I was completely in the dark. I felt suffocated. I felt lonely. This was my life.

Historical Note:
There are 3.6 million people of Chinese origin living in the United States. The largest concentrations are in Boston, MA; Flushing, Queens, and New York City, NY; San Francisco, Los Angeles, San Diego, and Sacramento, CA; Washington. DC; Houston and Plano, TX; Seattle, WA; Chicago, IL; Philadelphia, PA; Portland, OR; and Las Vegas, NV.

In China I came from a high place where everyone knew me. I was a doctor, the head of a department in a hospital, and I owned my own business. I was very successful. Here no one knew me and I didn't know anyone. It was terrible. In China we have an expression that going to America is like going to a second countryside. The first countryside was during the Cultural Revolution. This was the "Pacific Countryside." Both times I started out with enthusiasm and hope, but both times turned out much harder than I had imagined.

I called home a lot, but I didn't tell them about my life here. I only told them the interesting things, like learning English or taking the driver's test. Many times I wanted to cry, but I couldn't. When the phone bill came at the end of the month, my husband was really angry, even though the bill was under $100. This made me very sad. After this incident, I stopped making phone calls to my family; I only wrote letters.

After Thanksgiving, my husband bought me a used car so I could drive myself to school. One day while I was backing up in the parking lot of my school, I accidentally hit a car. My husband became angry and told me that the man might sue me because I didn't have my license. I was so scared that I decided not to return to that school, which made me feel even more suffocated. But I was determined to go to school, so one day after my husband had left for work, I drove his new Mazda without his permission to find another adult school. I was looking for the gate of the school when I hit a lamp pole. My air bags went off. The police and ambulance came. The car was totaled. My husband yelled at me: "Why can't you wait to go to school?" I told him I couldn't wait to start my life. I told him that his house was like a prison. I knew that the accident was my fault, but what angered me was that he didn't understand why I needed to go to school, and he never asked me if I had any injuries.

After that incident, my husband refused to talk with me. My only thought was that I wanted to die. I didn't eat or sleep for three days. After the third day, I fainted and was taken to the hospital. I was in the hospital for two hours and the bill was $1,500, which is 12,000 Chinese yen. I was shocked. People here pay a lot of money for health care. In China this same hospital stay would have cost maybe 100 Chinese yen or $10. Even though medical costs have gone up over the past ten years, quality health care is still affordable in China. The cost of an average doctor visit is at the most $3, and a visit with a specialist costs $10.

My husband got angrier and angrier. He said that I should pay him back. I didn't bring money to the United States because he told me that his salary could support us. When we were in China, he used my money, so I thought that in the beginning I could rely on him. He was my husband. He had a responsibility to support me. This is my culture. Inside my heart I felt very bad. After that

Face is very important in China. Without face, you should die.

incident I knew our marriage was a mistake, but I couldn't divorce him because if I did, my visa status would change, and I couldn't go back to China like a loser. Most Chinese never come here. They think if you come here, you must make life better. Face is very important in China. Without face, you should die. This is a powerful idea, formed by thousands of years of tradition. Wherever you go, whatever you do, you must be successful so that when you go back home you will bring something successful back. I am tied to the people back home because I am a part of them and they are a part of me, so if I don't succeed, it brings shame to my family and friends.

From that point on, I knew I could only depend on myself. I told myself that I was

. . . if I don't succeed, it brings shame to my family and friends.

going to make it in America, step by step. I was going to do everything I could to make it here. I went back to night school and started looking for jobs in the Chinese newspapers. My first job interview was in a cosmetic store. I was so excited. I brought all of my certificates from China with me. They didn't care about any of my certificates and didn't offer me the job, but they did ask me to buy $100 worth of cosmetics. I went on several more interviews before I realized that I needed to go to cosmetology school to get a license.

The school told me that I didn't have to take any classes because in China I had my own school and business, but they needed proof of my certificates and medical diplomas. I also had to take a class, which cost $1000, to help prepare me to take the cosmetology exam, which I had to pass to get a license. I borrowed $500 from my husband and asked my mother to send the rest.

Every night after I finished my homework for night school, I studied for my cosmetology exam until 2 a.m. The Chinese/English electronic dictionary I brought from China became my teacher and support. Since my husband didn't want to tutor me in English and I had no friends to study with, the only thing I could do was to memorize everything. The entire exam was in English.

In December 1999, almost a year and a half after I arrived in this country, I took the cosmetology test to get my license. I took the test with fifty-six men and women from all parts of the world: Africa, Mexico, Europe, and Japan. In the morning, we took the practical test, which included facials, hair, make-up and nails; and in the afternoon, we took the written test. Later that same day we got the results. Only seven people passed. Most had taken the test many times before, so when they found out they had passed, they were crying, clapping, jumping up and down, and holding each other. When I passed the test, I felt that I was starting my new life in the United States.

While I was in school, I continued looking for jobs. I had one really funny experience. I found an advertisement in the paper for a masseuse job at a clinic. I brought all my certificates with me. I drove around and around the block several times but couldn't find the clinic. There were only condos. When I finally found the place, it was not like a clinic and the people didn't show any interest in my certificates. I immediately became suspicious. A woman invited me in, and as we were talking, I looked up and saw a sexy girl coming down the stairs wearing a skimpy bra and shorts. I asked the person what kind of clinic it was. "We are not a clinic," she told me. "We only do massages." I understood pretty quickly that they weren't offering "real" massages. I knew these places were not legal. I felt scared and ran out.

I finally found a job in a salon in San Gabriel Valley three days a week doing facials and hair. My boss was Chinese so language was not a problem, and I was able to use my experience to make the spa better. My base salary was $30 a day for ten hours plus tips. The first time I received my $50 check, I felt so happy. Later I got a job at a newer salon that was bigger and more fashionable. I decided to work for the new salon three days a week. The boss set up a massage room especially for me. Unfortunately, I no longer had any time to go to school; I was working six days a week at two salons from 9 a.m. to 7 p.m. or later. In October of 1999, I quit one of my two jobs to work at a salon in Los Angeles, and then in May 2000, after I got my cosmetology license, I started working at the Los Angeles salon full time.

By this time, even though I had been in this country for almost two years, I had only been in school a total of two months and had almost no English speaking skills. I had learned simple things like how to greet people and how to say my name and address, but I couldn't have a simple conversation, or answer a simple question. I had done this work professionally in China, but here I couldn't use my knowledge to explain the benefits of what I was doing or even give my customers simple directions. I had to point and gesture whenever I wanted them to move up

Actually, I felt the same about Americans. I thought they all looked alike too.

or down on the massage table. I must have said "sorry" and "thank you" hundreds of times every day. It was terrible.

I remember one day my boss called me over to talk with a customer who was very angry. She had had her eyebrows waxed the day before, but she didn't know who had done the work. She pointed at me even though I hadn't worked on her. I guess she thought that all Asians looked alike. Actually, I felt the same about Americans. I thought they all looked alike too. She took off her glasses and showed us her eyebrows, which were slightly burned, and she threatened to call a lawyer. I didn't know what was going on. I was unable to explain that I was the wrong person. I couldn't defend myself. I was so scared I couldn't sleep at all that night.

When I didn't have customers, I studied English. I took out children's books from the library, like *The Babysitter's Club* by Ann M. Martin, and I think I read all of Judy Blume's books. I remember being so surprised that the children in the books earned their own spending money. That would never happen in China. I carried my electronic dictionary at all times to help with the new vocabulary. It often took a day to read one page. After I had been at the salon for a few months, one of my customers offered to teach me English at her house on my day off.

The day I met this woman, life became brighter. She gave me hope that I could make it here. In my first class, I asked her to write down all the words and

Xidan, her mother and son, Hong Bin, in Chongqing, 2000.

56

phrases I needed to do my job, like "lie down" or "move up a little." Then I went home and memorized everything. She told me to use English with my customers as much as I could and ask them to correct me, which they always did.

My teacher also helped me study for my citizenship test. I loved learning about American history and culture, so different from China's. America has a short but interesting history. People from all over the world have come here. There are many languages and cultures, but sometimes I wonder what is American culture? China is 5,000 years old, and for the most part, our traditions have been continuous. They have been passed on from generation to generation. Because of that, change comes very slowly. China is like a large tree with very deep roots. Sometimes these traditions become too controlling. For example, here when I divorced my husband, nobody cared. Nobody even asked about it. In China, everyone would care. Everyone knows everything about your life, no matter how personal. There is no privacy.

My Son Comes to the United States

In March 2000, I went back to China to visit my family and complete paperwork to bring my son to the United States to live with me. It was hard being in China because I missed my old life. I remembered how important I had been and how needed I was. But I couldn't stay; I had to come back. Naturally, my mother asked me how I was doing, but I didn't tell her about the sad and difficult times. I didn't want to worry her.

Like all Chinese kids his age, my son was excited to come here. He wanted to go to the university, and he thought he could get a good education here. Even though the Chinese government is building more universities, there aren't enough for the number of students who want to go. Like most Chinese kids, my son is a very good student. Chinese parents force their kids to get a good education. We tell them that if they get a good education, they will have a good future. We tell our kids that their only job is to study, study and study some more. No games. No fun. Just study. That is why Chinese students do well here. They're good at being students. But after graduation, they have a hard time fitting into society.

Before he left China, I had a serious conversation with him. I told him not to imagine that the United States was a paradise because the truth was that life here was tough for immigrants, and that he needed to prepare himself psychologically. I didn't want him to come here and be disappointed. I told him that my life here was different than in China. I told him that my little salary was not enough to completely support him and that he would need to learn how to take care of himself. I told him that here if you are dependent on your parents, you will feel shame. I wanted my son to be prepared.

After I returned from China, I bought a condominium so that my son could have his own room. I also prepared a room for my mom, hoping she would one day come to the United States. But she never came. She died in China on January 28, 2008. The condominium was in Monterey Park, which is about 70 percent Chinese, so life was much easier for me. I was around Chinese people. I could walk to restaurants and stores. Many of the people I met in the restaurants became my customers. The best part was that I could use my language.

My husband didn't think that my son should live with us. He said that in the United States when kids turned eighteen, they live by themselves. I told him that this was not the Chinese way. My son arrived in Los Angeles on July 6, 2000, two years and two days after I arrived. When he got off the plane, he was wearing expensive clothing and shoes. I told him that if he wanted to fit in here, he couldn't dress that way, and I went out immediately to buy him less expensive clothing and shoes.

My son adjusted to life here quickly. The first week he passed the written test for his driver's license, and the second week he found a job in a Chinese restaurant as a bus boy. He had never worked before, and in the beginning it was like a new game to him. He didn't know how hard it would be. He often worked twelve hours without a break and would come home very tired. But he learned a lot of skills. He started as a bus boy and then worked as a cook and later a waiter.

His goal was to go to college. At first he enrolled in computer classes in a private school, and after he received his green card, he began taking classes at East Los Angeles College. After two years, he transferred to the University of California at Riverside where he received his Bachelor's degree in math. After that, he went to the University of Texas at Austin for his Master's degree. He now attends Columbia University where he is working on his Ph.D. My son is a very good student. He has received straight "A's" in all the classes he has taken here.

Reflections

I always like to ask my customers about their dreams for the future. What do they want to achieve in their lives? What is important to them? Many tell me that they want to find a handsome, rich man who will buy them a nice house, a new car and beautiful dresses. They want someone to take care of them. This surprises me. They don't have a larger dream or goal for their lives. They don't have a sense of nationalism or feel obligated to do things for their country. They have infinite freedoms, but they don't have any sublime ideals. This is so different from China. From an early age, children are taught in school that their lives must have a higher purpose. Success is when you make a big change in your country. Mao didn't make a lot of money, but he changed the whole country. He made

They have infinite freedoms, but they don't have any sublime ideals.

58

people's lives better. That is success. This is also the meaning of face. When my mother died, she gave her body to science. That is face.

Another thing I noticed was how different families are here. In China, families are very close. I don't see that here. There is no mutual concern or support, and as a result, their relationships with their families are distant. I have young customers who move out of the house when they are eighteen. This is too young. They live tough lives. They work to pay for rent and food. They can't even afford to go to school. This would never happen in China. In China, parents have the responsibility to take care of their children until they can take care of themselves, no matter what age. Kids are totally dependent on their parents. They can't even do the simplest things, like cook or do laundry. Their only job is to study. This has always been our culture, but now because of the one-child policy, each child has six parents to take care of him or her—the mother and father and two sets of grandparents. The father helps the child with homework, and the grandparent peels the grapes and feeds them to the child.

When the parents are old, the children take care of them. There is a saying in China, "Rest your kids for your retirement." Until my mother died, I spoke with her every Thursday night, and my brother visited her every day. She needed the warmth and conversation. I have a customer who is eighty-nine years old. Every week she comes to me for a massage. I have become the person she depends upon because her daughter lives far away. Women like her need and deserve more attention and care paid to them.

China is a like a sleeping lion that has awakened.

While many of the old traditions remain in China, change is happening very fast. China is like a sleeping lion that has awakened. Thirty years ago, we didn't even have radios in China. Our movies were old, and our clothes not fashionable. When relatives brought new things to China, it was very exciting. Now change is happening very fast. The economy has experienced rapid growth. People from all over the world are begining to start businesses. I am very proud of that, but I worry that some of the changes have happened too fast and that there hasn't been time to evaluate them. People's thinking has changed. China is becoming more like the United States. People only care about money. Their dreams are not about the good of the country, but about themselves. I don't think this is good. My generation had the responsibility to make our country stronger. We had important ideals. We had the "hot blood of patriotism." This generation feels none of that.

No matter how much China has changed, no matter how much China has become like the United States, Chinese people still come together around a common purpose. You could see this in the devastating earthquake that hit China on May 12, 2008. Everyone helped. Everyone came together. Immediately the government asked every city to set up a collection area. The army responded quickly.

Famous people like Yao Ming and Jet Li set up foundations, and other people gave money. Chinese people are proud of that.

You could also see this pride during the recent Olympics in China. We wanted to show our country to the world. For many years China had been closed to the rest of the world. Most people thought China was poor, with no education or human rights. We wanted to show that it has a long history with many achievements. We also wanted to show that we want to live together in peace, with respect for all people. Chinese people, wherever they were in the world, watched the 2008 Olympics with pride.

My Life Today

I don't know if I will stay in the United States. I have made a life here. I like my job. I like making people feel beautiful and happy. But I miss the respect and recognition for who I am and what I've accomplished. It's just that I have always had a larger goal for my life. I would love to start my own business here, but that doesn't seem possible. My language is not good enough, and I don't have the funds I need. In China, I knew that if I worked hard, I could accomplish my goals. I just don't know how to do that here. Sometimes I feel sad. But I have friends around me who tell me never to give up my dream. In my heart, I never give up. That's my personality.

Ana's and Juanita's Stories

Ana Leiva was born on December 15, 1944, in the city of Santa Ana, El Salvador, which is in the north-west part of the country. After graduating from Escuela Normal (teaching college) in 1965, she began her career as an elementary school teacher,

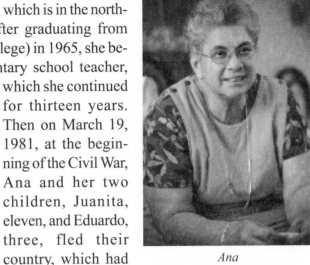

Ana

which she continued for thirteen years. Then on March 19, 1981, at the beginning of the Civil War, Ana and her two children, Juanita, eleven, and Eduardo, three, fled their country, which had become so dangerous that every day they feared for their lives. Her husband Miguel joined her fifteen days later. Here are Ana's and Juanita's stories.

Juanita

Historical Note:

The Civil War in El Salvador, which lasted from 1980 to 1992, had its roots in the economic and social inequalities that defined the country for much of the nineteenth century. During that time, fourteen families owned 99 percent of the wealth in the country, their interests protected by a series of military governments that maintained the status quo through a campaign of intimidation and repression. There were many challenges to this power, but most were met with overwhelming force. In 1969, El Salvador went to war with Honduras in what is called "The Football War." The war, which left the Salvadoran economy devastated, helped create the conditions for the rise of opposition parties and guerilla armies resulting in the twelve-year El Salvador Civil War.

Ana Begins Her Story

My Parents

My father, Ricardo Aguirre, was born in Santa Ana, El Salvador, in 1914. He was the oldest of five children. He loved reading and learning and probably could have become a teacher or lawyer if he had continued in school, but he only went

Ricardo Aguirre, Ana's father. He had just returned from Panama, 1943.

for six years, which was the basic education at that time. After sixth grade, most children either learned a trade or found a job. My father went to work for the city newspaper *Diario de Occidente* as a typesetter.

In the early 1940s when my father was about twenty-eight, he and his brother Frank went to Panama for a few years to work on the Panama Canal. As the oldest child, my father had to step up and take care of the family because his father had left them behind to live with another woman. After my father and his brother came back from Panama, my Uncle Frank moved to New York, where he opened a photo studio and started sending money to my grandmother, which she used to open a little community store. She sold everything—soap, spices, bread and candies. She added a soda shop where she sold juices and *paletas* (ices). She had a large neighborhood clientele.

My mother, Salvadora Morán de Santillana, was born in the Department of Santa Ana, outside of the city of Santa Ana, in a little town called Chalchuapa near Tazumal, the Mayan ruins. She had three sisters and one brother. My mother only went to school for one year because her mother thought that if she could read and write, she would send love letters to boys. She always regretted not going further in school. My mother's family owned a small plot of land outside the city where they planted crops like tobacco and different fruits and vegetables. One of their neighbors wanted to buy their land, but her mother (my grandmother) didn't want to sell. To scare her into selling the land, the neighbor chopped off her braids with a machete. He intended to chop off her head but only got the braids. After that my grandmother sold their land.

My mother's parents split up when she was ten years old, and she and one of her sisters went to live with their father. A year later he died, and my grandmother took my mother to San Salvador, the capitol, to live with another family as their *hija de crianza,* which was like legal slavery. This was a common practice at this time. Because of poverty, people wanted to have fewer mouths to feed and children to clothe. These girls had no rights, and many were sexually abused by men who lived in the houses. When my mother was thirteen, the nephew of the owner of the house attempted to rape her. She was saved when a friend came to the door and yelled my mother's name.

My mother had only lived at the house a few months when my grandmother died, leaving my mom an orphan. She eventually went to live with her sister in

Santa Ana, but that was difficult. My mother and her sister were like oil and water. My mother was easygoing and always got along with everyone, but her sister was like their mother, impulsive with an explosive temper.

Most women in our culture are dominated by "machismo," which is when men think they can run everything.

When my mother was eighteen, she met my father, Ricardo. My father's family didn't like my mother because, as an orphan, she couldn't bring a dowry to the marriage. This practice comes from colonial times when women "came to the table" with more than themselves, but since my mother was an orphan, she only came with herself. My parents never married, but they were together for eight years and had two children. My mom lived with my sister Margarita and me at her house, and my father lived at his mom's house and would come after work to see us and then go back to his mother's. Like a lot of men of his time, he was a mama's boy who didn't want to take on too much responsibility.

My mother was always independent and far ahead of her time. For one thing, she smoked, and women just didn't do that in my country at that time. She also liked to work and make her own money, and she never wanted to rely on a husband to support her. My mom taught me how to fight and get ahead in difficult times. Maybe because she was orphaned at such an early age, she wanted to make sure I could take care of myself. Most women in our culture are dominated by "machismo," which is when men think they can run everything. Salvadoran mothers teach their daughters to be submissive and to serve their husband. Even if their marriage is not working, they can never get a divorce. They have to suffer. My mom was different.

My mother was a very good business woman. I remember going with her to the train station to buy fresh fruits, vegetables, eggs and chicken to sell house-to-house. She also made *chilate*, which is a cultural drink, our version of a high tea. It's a drink made of roasted corn and spices like anise, sassafrás, all spice, and ginger. You drink it with sweet foods to wash away the sweetness. She would set up chairs and tables around a pit where the *chilate* would cook. On Sundays, my mother would go to the outskirts of Santa Ana to sell

Salvadora Moran de Santillana, 1978.

63

I would read anything I could get my hands on—
comic books, magazines and novels.
I especially liked biographies, like those
of Madame Curie and Florence Nightingale.

soap, which at that time was made out of lard and ash. She always worked. She never rested.

When I was eight years old, my parents split up. My father told my mother that she could keep me because I was the older of the two daughters, but that he wouldn't leave her alone until she gave him my little sister Margarita. Growing up, I always wanted to be near my little sister, and every time I visited her at my father's house, I cried. My father's mother (my grandmother) would scold me and tell me not to come if I was going to cry. I never felt comfortable at my father's house, but he always tried to make sure my sister and I saw each other. When my sister was in high school and she wasn't doing well in algebra, my father would send her to me for help. It wasn't about teaching her; it was about spending time together.

My sister and I are completely different. She is outgoing like our mother, always needing to be the center of attention. I was always more like my father, who loved reading and talking with people. I would read anything I could get my hands on—comic books, magazines and novels. I especially liked biographies, like those of Madame Curie and Florence Nightingale. I liked the fact that they were strong women and had been successful in their careers.

When I was eight years old, my mother met Ricardo Santillana, who became my stepfather. I guess she liked men named Ricardo because my father's name was also Ricardo. My stepfather and I were never close, but as I got older, he became a very important part of my life. He and my mother had a good relationship, and he also had a cordial relationship with my father, which was the exception to the rule. My mom and stepfather had five children together, four boys and one girl. My half-sister was born when I was twenty. I was like a second mother to my half-siblings. In my culture, it is custom that the oldest child takes care of the younger children, so when my mom went to work, I was in charge. I felt that was my obligation to the family.

I loved school and got excellent grades, but I was often bored and when I finished my work, I would make trouble for the teachers. When I finished the sixth grade, I took a test to be admitted to the Instituto Nacional de Santa Ana (INSA). I remember going to the school to see if I had passed the test. There was a long list of names, beginning with the student with the highest score. First I looked at the middle of the list and then the end. I couldn't find my name. Then suddenly there it was at the top of the list. I had the highest score. The day I enrolled in INSA, all the teachers congratulated my mother. She was so proud.

When I was growing up, Santa Ana was a beautiful and tranquil place. There were four churches in the center of the city, one for each direction—north, south, east and west. Two had parks in front of them. Our main cathedral looked like Saint Patrick's Cathedral in New York City. People with money lived in barrios (neighborhoods) in the center of Santa Ana around the main plaza, the cathedral, and the park; and the poor people lived in barrios around the outskirts of the city. Each barrio had a different name: San Rafael, Santa Bárbara, San Lorenzo, Santa Lucía, Colón, Barrio Nuevo and Santa Cruz. My barrio was San Rafael.

Catedral de Santa Ana, 1998.

We lived in a *mesón* in San Rafael. Each family lived in one room with a small kitchen; the rooms were built around a square. The bathroom, sink, showers and courtyard were in the middle of the square so everyone could share them. My mom, brothers, sisters and I slept in the *mesón*. My stepfather worked at a mill near our house, and on most nights he would sleep there and come home to eat with the family. This was more convenient because people would arrive at the mill early in the morning to grind their coffee beans and also corn to make *masa*. *Masa* is used to make many things, such as tortillas, *pasteles de carne* and tamales. They would also grind spices, tomatoes to make salsa, and the filling for *pupusas*. *Pupusas* are typically filled with fried beans, *chicharrón* (fried pork) and *queso con loroco* (cheese and a fragrant plant). The mill was an important part of everyday life. It was where people ground their food to eat or to sell.

I helped out at the mill whenever my stepfather

Historical Note:
Santa Ana is located in the northwest part of El Salvador. Today it has a population of almost 275,000 and is the second largest city in the country. San Salvador, the nation's capital, is the largest city.

> *At that time if you were sent to jail because you were against the government, you were treated worse than if you were a criminal.*

needed me. He never learned to read or write, but he wanted to be kept up to date on all the news, especially international and national news, so he would set aside bundles of newspapers for me to read to him whenever I went to the mill. Even though he couldn't read or write, he was great at math and could make calculations in his head. It was incredible. When my stepfather got together with my mom, he was working for someone else, but a short time later he bought one mill, and during the next nine years, he bought seven or eight other mills. He was very methodical, and my mom was a hard worker, so between the two of them they were able to save. Their dream was to earn enough money to buy a little house, and when I was seventeen, they finally did.

My stepfather was very involved with one of the anti-government political parties in El Salvador, the PDC (Partido Demócrata Cristiano). Sometimes at midnight he would leave the house to plaster anti-government posters on the walls in the city, and when the Cuban revolution started, he would turn on the radio very low each night at midnight to listen to Fidel Castro's speeches. This was dangerous at that time. The government was always keeping their ears and eyes open. He got into trouble once in about 1964. The teachers were meeting at a construction site near where we lived to plan a strike, and he went to listen to what they were saying. The police came, rounded up people and took them to jail, including my stepfather. We had to go and talk with a friend who was able to get my stepfather out of jail. It was very delicate. At that time if you were sent to jail because you were against the government, you were treated worse than if you were a criminal.

Miguel, Ana's husband, standing at the door of his bus in Santa Ana, El Salvador, 1980.

Meeting My Husband

I met my husband through one of his friends who was going out with my cousin. Pretty soon the four of us started to double-date. Every weekend we went to the movies,

66

which were the only source of entertainment in the city, and on school days in the afternoon when my classes ended, he would always be waiting for me. I liked him because he was humble, got along well with people, and said "yes" to everything I wanted. He also liked that I was smart and even helped me study for my exams. Even though my husband only finished the sixth grade, he never felt intimidated by me.

My husband's father grew up in Guatemala and fled to El Salvador because of his political involvement in his country. As a young man, he spent many years in prison for his politics, and according to family folklore, his sister broke him out of jail. His family had a lot of money, so when he arrived in El Salvador

Ana and Miguel on their wedding day, October 12, 1968.

with his wife, he was able to buy a large home, like a plantation, with a lot of cattle. When his wife couldn't get pregnant, he had an affair with a young woman named Rita, who was their *hija de crianza*, and over the years they had six children together, including my father. When my husband was six years old, his father died, making his mother trustee of the inheritance, but his mother was very young and illiterate and her lover at the time convinced her to sign everything over to him. He swindled her out of everything.

Marriage and Children

My husband and I were married on October 12, 1968. It was a very exciting and emotional time. We went to San Salvador to buy all the wedding materials, appliqués, satin and fabric for my dress and my little sister's dress, which was like mine. One of my mother's friends made beautiful bouquets of natural flowers for my bridesmaids, and my cousin Juanita lent me her earrings and did my hair and make-up. In El Salvador, the bride selects a happily married woman to help her get ready.

We had a big traditional Catholic wedding with about 300 people. To this day I hear about people who were hurt that I didn't invite them. I had a maid of honor, bridesmaids and a ring bearer. My little sister accompanied the ring bearer. I had everything ready, but we forgot one thing—the traditional lasso, which is used to tie the couple together. In the middle of the ceremony, my mother had to rush out to buy one.

We had fattened up a pig, and the day of the wedding we killed and roasted it to make sandwiches. My stepfather's brother prepared drinks called *highballs*. It was a day with much activity. My house was full. I had so many gifts that I needed to borrow an extra table. Even after the wedding, my father brought over gifts from friends.

On August 12, 1969, ten months after our wedding, my daughter Juanita was born, and my son Eduardo was born eight years later on November 23, 1977. Between my two children, I gave birth to a daughter who was stillborn. When Juanita was eight months old, she developed polio. There was a polio epidemic sweeping the country at that time, and many children died. Thankfully, my daughter's polio was not as strong as others. After she became sick, my husband and I focused on her completely. Machismo took a back seat. My husband took her to rehabilitation, bathed her, changed her diapers, and was always very patient with her. Sometimes when Juanita was sick, he would be so tired that he would bump into the furniture. When he got too tired, I took over. My husband was an exception to the cultural norm. Most men didn't help with their children.

For several years, he made good money by working in a body shop, but when the owners stopped paying their workers on time, he quit and went to work as a bus driver. At first he worked for someone, but then he and a group of friends bought their own bus route. He was one of the first principal players to set up a *cooperativa* (a cooperative). They started with a few buses and ended up owning thirty-five, all of them in good condition. When we left El Salvador to come to the United States, he had to give up his share of the cooperative. The men who stayed are all millionaires.

My Teaching Career

From the time I was ten years old, I knew that I wanted to be a teacher. I always loved to play school with the kids in the *mesón*. I would get all the kids together, sit them down, give them paper and tell them what to write. I would read stories with them and ask questions about what we had read.

In 1962, when I was eighteen, I entered Escuela Normal Capitán

Third-year students in El Salvador's Escuela Normal, 1965. Ana is in the top row left.

General Gerardo Barrios (named after the president of El Salvador from 1859 to 1863) to prepare to become a teacher. I remember that I was excited and scared. During the opening session, all the students were asked to come up on stage, and when my best friend Ana María and I went up to the stage, some of the students singled us out for being tall. They called us the "Twin Towers," because we were the tallest students. Most people in El Salvador are short. We were the exceptions.

I finished Escuela Normal when I was twenty-one and spent the next two years looking for a teaching job. During those two years, the first teachers union was organized, ANDES 21 de Junio. ANDES stands for the National Association of Salvadoran Educators, and June 21 is the day the union was formed. Before the establishment of ANDES, the government was happy with teachers because they were quiet and did everything the government wanted, but when the teachers began to rise up against the government, everything changed and the government turned on the teachers.

ANDES organized their first strike around the time I had graduated from college and was looking for my first teaching job. Their demands were that the government offer teachers medical insurance, which teachers didn't have even though they were public servants. They also asked that the retirement age be cut from forty years of service to thirty. The strike was successful and they won both demands. After the strike, ANDES began supporting other labor unions, which got them into a lot of trouble with the government. Unions were always against the government. In 1971, ANDES called for a national strike, and all the schools in the country were shut down for about three months. Every day we picketed and went to meetings. We went on strike with a lot of fear. Participating in a strike was dangerous.

In 1968, I began working as a third-grade teacher at an elementary school in the city of Santa Ana. The school served about 300 kids from mostly working-class families. I was lucky because there were a lot of experienced teachers at that school. Many taught at the INSA, sometimes two times a day, before and after school. I taught there for about six months.

Teachers at Escuela Rural Mixta del Cantón Ayutepeque in 1971. Ana is in the first row on the right.

*Despite the hard conditions, my students
were always neat and organized.
They cherished their education, as did their parents.*

My second teaching job was at a school in the countryside about twenty minutes from Santa Ana called Escuela Rural Mixta del Cantón Ayutepeque. I taught at this school for eight years. The families of my students were very poor. They had no running water. In the summer the families had to buy their water from the water truck, which was very expensive. The families worked on a coffee farm planting coffee and shade trees, and they made a little extra money by selling leftover coffee and tree branches. Most of my students worked to help support the family and missed months of school. Most came back to school in March instead of January because they had to work during the coffee season, and some didn't show up until after Easter. But always when the students came back to school, they would put in a lot of effort to make up for lost time. Despite the hard conditions, my students were always neat and organized. They cherished their education, as did their parents.

When I started working at that school, I had 100 students in my class. Some of my students had to sit on the floor because there weren't enough desks, and I never had enough books or supplies for all the students. In El Salvador, families have to purchase supplies, and these families didn't have the money to do this. But my students and their parents were resourceful and used whatever they had around them to learn. One time I was teaching about insects and the students brought in insects from home I had never seen before. In the United States, there is an abundance of resources, but it seems that the students waste their time. Perhaps this is because students don't value what they have.

I was passionate about teaching, and I had high standards for my students. My goal was to give my students confidence. I

Ana with her fourth-grade students from Escuela Rural Mixta del Cantón Ayutepeque, 1971. Carlos Zeledón is on the right behind the student with the dark shirt.

had students who were good at school and could have become something, but they were really poor and didn't have the opportunity to go further. But they always tried to do their best. Most stopped at the sixth grade. I never knew of any who went on to college. I had one student whose name was Carlos Zeledón. He was very dedicated to his studies. He was nice and respectful and was the first to raise his hand and volunteer to help. He was definitely smart enough to go to college. It just wasn't possible. It was such a shame.

After eight years, I found a half-time job back in Santa Ana so I could be closer to my home and spend more time with my children. Even though it was more convenient, I missed teaching at my former school. I loved teaching those children.

Life during the Civil War

When the Civil War started, life became very dangerous. You would find decapitated bodies everywhere. You would find dead bodies in dumpsters. There were shootouts when you least expected them. Stray bullets would kill innocent people. Every week, when Juanita and I took the bus to the capital to see her doctor for her polio rehabilitation treatments, I would go with fear that something would happen to us. The government set up check points throughout the

Historical Note:
The Civil War, which officially began on January 10, 1981, was fought between the Salvadoran military dictatorship and the Farabundo Martí National Liberation Movement (FMLN). The FMLN, a unified opposition movement consisting of five guerilla groups, was formed on October 10, 1980. The assassination of the Archbishop of San Salvador, Oscar Arnulfo Romero, on March 24, 1980, helped spark the Civil War. He was one of the most important and vocal critics of the United States' support of the military government. At his funeral, government snipers killed forty-two mourners. Then on December 2, 1980, four American churchwomen were raped and murdered, igniting massive public demonstrations. Many people believed that the government was responsible.

The Civil War ended in January 1992 with the establishment of a new constitution. The constitution established the FMLN as a legal political party, regulated the armed forces, and created a civilian police force. The Civil War resulted in the deaths of 75,000 civilians and the disappearance of another 8,000, many at the hands of the government-sponsored "death squads."

city. Many times they would stop the bus, force everyone off, and look through our handbags and backpacks for weapons. Sometimes they would demand that the bus drivers give them money or their bus. If the drivers refused, they would burn the bus. Many bus drivers were killed trying to protect their bus.

The unions began organizing a series of one-day strikes in San Salvador, and many of the people who marched in those demonstrations would be found the next day burned beyond recognition. One of my cousins went out to a park after curfew and the government killed him. He was twenty-eight. Another step-cousin, German Santillana, disappeared completely. He was twenty-four at the time, and we never saw him again. The government only killed young people.

German Santillana, Ana's step-cousin who disappeared in 1981 during the Civil War.

We never knew what would happen from day to day. A person could die not because they belonged to an organization, but just as a side effect of war. A person could be walking down the street, and a bomb could go off. This affects you psychologically.

We were worried about our children's future. There was a possibility they would grow up without parents.

By the time classes started in the summer of 1981, life had become even more dangerous. The government-sponsored "death squads" were killing teachers in their own homes, and many top-ranked members of ANDES had to flee the country because they were on a list of teachers who were condemned to die. At school you had to have a lot of tact. There were teachers against the strikes and teachers for the strikes. There was a group called AMAD that supported the government. They could finger you and you would be killed. It was best to keep your mouth shut. We lived in a constant state of fear and nervousness. The government would pull teachers who were riding to demonstrations off of buses, and then the teachers would disappear.

In January 1981, the guerillas attacked the *cuartel*, which was the military headquarters in our city, and burned their military artillery supply. Shots and bombs went off constantly. We couldn't leave our house for four days. We learned by word of mouth and the radio that there were bodies decomposing all over the streets. Flies were everywhere, and stray dogs were eating the bodies. We would hear horrible noises, and we didn't know what was happening. There was no transportation. Nothing was running. We didn't know what was happening with our relatives. People who couldn't get home were hiding all over the city. My husband wasn't home. He was working the afternoon shift that day. Usually when he worked that shift, he would get home by 11 p.m., but because of the fighting, he couldn't move across the city. He drove the bus back to where the buses were parked and stayed with the bus and all the passengers until the next morning. We couldn't communicate with anyone. We didn't have a telephone. We couldn't open the door to anyone. We just prayed that everyone was safe.

My husband and I had been thinking about leaving the country for about a year or so, but when the situation became dire, we decided that we had to leave. We were worried about our children's future. There was a possibility they would grow up without parents. We didn't know what the future would bring, but we knew we didn't want to live in fear.

When things got harried, I called my sister Margarita in New Jersey to help us get a visa so we could leave. She had moved to the United States with my father's family in 1970. The minute she became a citizen and could help us get a visa, we left El Salvador and came here. Margarita was a registered nurse and was able to convince one of her doctor friends to write a letter saying that Juanita needed an operation on her leg because of her polio. That letter made it easier to get a visa, and once we were in the U.S., my sister knew she could get us residency status.

Juanita's Story

I was a happy kid. My life was about the smells of my grandma's cooking, learning from her, and talking about life with Manuel. Manuel was a friend of my mom's stepfather, and when my mom got married, Manuel came to live with us. My mom used to joke that Manuel was her dowry. He was very political, and every day we would read the newspaper and listen to the radio together.

School was everything. I read a lot. I really liked Little Women, *and I especially loved the character Jo. She was independent and strong, and she always spoke her mind.*

Juanita, ten years old.

Growing up, I always knew I had a disability. I had to go to rehabilitation three days a week for painful therapy. I knew I had physical limitations, but my friends have always liked me for who I am. It didn't really click until I was eight or nine years old. I remember that I was walking in the city and saw a reflection of a girl who was limping in one of the buildings. I realized that the girl was me. My parents never focused on the fact that I was disabled. They never said, "Your leg defines you."

One of my first memories of the Civil War was when I went to a meeting at the plaza next to City Hall with my mother and one of her younger brothers. I was five or six at the time. We had just come from bringing my father food while he was on his bus route. It was night and lights were focused on the man who was speaking. Suddenly the lights were turned off. It was completely dark. Everyone was afraid. The feeling was palpable. Then I heard shots. I remember my mom took one hand and my uncle took the other and we started to run. I remember looking up and seeing all these dark shadows running. I remember thinking—we could get killed. I could

I remember hearing, "They're coming; they're coming," and an electric current of fear ran through the house.

sense that my mom was tense and fearful because her hold on my hand got progressively tighter. I knew that if my mom was feeling fear, I should be afraid. After the lights came back on, my mom remembered that we had left my dad's lunchbox behind, and her fear of being shot turned into fear of my dad finding out she had put me in danger by being in the plaza. When we went back to where we had been standing, there was the lunch box. We never mentioned this to my father. This experience is sealed in my mind.

After that, things just started exploding. Shots were being fired everywhere. Bombs were going off everywhere. You could hear them from my house, which was in the outskirts of the city. My brother and I slept on a pile of blankets next to our parents' bed because they were afraid that a stray bullet could go through the walls and kill us. We were in constant fear that whenever my parents went out, they might not come back. They could be shopping for food, and someone could be chasing a guerilla, and they could be caught in the crossfire and be killed.

I had a friend whose sister disappeared one night. She was standing on the corner talking to a boy. They were just teenagers who were flirting with each other. Someone had fingered the boy saying he might be involved with the guerillas. A couple of days later they found her body and she looked like she was pregnant. Her mom said she wasn't pregnant; she was a skinny little girl. They opened up her body and found the head of the boy in her belly. They had tortured this girl. It was horrible.

I had another friend who saw her mom killed right in front of her. Her mom was a teacher and so was her father, but her father wasn't at home that day. My friend, her mom and her brothers and sisters were at home. The death squads tortured her in the living room in front of her children. Then they shot her in the head and killed her. My friend became catatonic.

I remember the day we burned the books. I was eight or nine years old. The government had a program called a cateo *(random search) where the government would close off blocks in the neighborhood and go house to house looking for evidence that you belonged to a guerilla cell or were against the government. As soon as people found out about the* cateo, *they would tell their neighbors, who would in turn tell their neighbors until everyone in the community knew.*

My dad wasn't at home that day because he was working, but the rest of us were home—my mother, my grandmother who lived with us, my brother who was really little and Manuel who lived with us. I remember hearing, "They're coming; they're coming," and an electric current of fear ran through the house. Everyone was hyper. Manuel pulled out our "subversive" books that were hidden between the tiles in the ceiling, and my grandmother went to work making masa, *needed to make tortillas, to give us an excuse to make a fire. I remember the knock at the door, which was the one thing you didn't want to hear. I remember the black military boots walking by. Manuel was sitting reading the newspaper and greeted them politely as my grandmother stirred the pot; all the time the books were burning right under the tortillas.*

We knew there was something horrible going on, but no one would talk about it. It was dangerous even for kids to talk about political things because you never knew whom you could trust. You didn't know who would turn around and stab you in the back. One time my mom was called to school because I accused someone of being a guerilla. We were all against the government. We all wanted to be political but we couldn't. It was self- preservation. If you defied the government in any way, there would be repercussions. You would hear at school that so-and-so's brother got kidnapped. We heard about families that had been killed for helping someone running from the government. You couldn't trust anyone.

Ana Continues Her Story

March 16, 1981: The Day I left El Salvador with My Children.

The day we left I felt a great amount of pain because we were a close-knit family. My husband couldn't come with us but joined us fifteen days later. I remember looking at my house and thinking, God only knows what will happen to us. We were leaving behind everything we had worked for, everything we had achieved. I didn't know if we would ever come back. But you always try and protect your family, and living through a war increased my desire to protect my family.

Historical Note:
Almost two million Salvadoran people live in the United States, mostly in Los Angeles. Also large communities live in Houston, Dallas, San Francisco, Long Island, Chicago and the greater Washington DC area.

We left quietly without telling anyone. We took only a few clothes and personal effects so no one would notice. I remember that my dad told my husband to bring a dictionary/encyclopedia (the Spanish name for this is *El Pequeño Larousse Ilustrado*) and some geography books to help us in the United States.

I imagined that the United States would be more developed than our own country and that everything would be bigger, brighter and grander. That is what I found. But what I didn't count on was the change in weather. It was so cold, much colder than our tropical climate. When my sister, Margarita, came to pick us up at the airport in New York, she brought coats and sweaters for all of us. Even with the heavy coat, I was so cold I thought I was naked. After this experience, whenever I thought winter was coming, I would panic. I hate the cold.

We lived in a small bedroom in my sister's house for the first year, and then moved downstairs to her basement, which was like a small apartment, for another three years. It felt strange living in her house. Even though we were sisters, we had never lived together growing up, so we were almost strangers. My family

Margarita (Ana's sister) and her husband Jorge Recinos, 1982. Taken by Ana's Uncle Frank.

was used to our home in El Salvador. It wasn't huge, but it was ours. We had privacy and we could watch whatever we wanted on television. At my sister's house, my husband, two kids and I lived in one room, and we had to watch what they wanted. I often felt sad because I had left my family and country behind. We were here, but we were always worried about family members left behind. Sometimes I would wake up crying because I had dreamt about my mother. Even though life was hard, I always tried to make things easier for my kids. I encouraged them to try new things, like different kinds of foods. Humor and fun helped a lot. We always tried to find the humor in everything. There is a saying in my country, "Bad time, good face." I was stunned when I saw how quickly and easily my kids adjusted to life here.

One of the good things that happened is that I spent the first couple of months with my father. That was a beautiful time. We talked about things we didn't talk about when I was a child. I told him I wished I had grown up with him, my mom and my sister. I asked him why he had fought for Margarita and not for me, why he didn't take both of us. I asked him if he fought for her because she was his daughter and I wasn't. He told me not to be ridiculous.

The hardest part of being here was not being able to work. When we came here, my son was just three years old, and my sister told me

Family photo, 1981.
Ana and Eduardo are in the front;
Juanita and Miguel in back.

that whatever I earned, I would spend on babysitters. I had been an independent woman in El Salvador. I earned my own money and spent it any way I wanted, but here since I didn't work, I felt dependent on my husband. That felt terrible. The good thing was that my husband found work in a body shop a week after we arrived. When he got his check, he told me to spend it as I saw fit. This was a big change. In El Salvador I never knew my husband's salary. He would give me money, but I never knew his salary. But here he would tell me, "Distribute the money any way you want; just give me some cash." My husband became closer to us as a family. In El Salvador he would go off with his friends, but when we got here, he helped out more. We would go to the market and do things around the house together. He looked inward. The social environment changed. In a way, it was a positive thing for our family. We all got closer. We had to work as a team.

Another hard thing for me was language. I remember feeling stupid because people would talk and talk and I couldn't understand one single word they were saying. I couldn't communicate with anyone. I would have to rely on Juanita to translate for me, which made me feel ignorant. I felt that I was an alien on another planet. This is the most horrible thing that can happen to a person. I would see children speaking and think, even the children know more than I do, and wonder, when will I understand one word they're saying? Even a little thing like going to

I would see children speaking and think, even the children know more than I do, and wonder, when will I understand one word they're saying?

the market became a big thing. One time I bought a jar of sour cream, and when I got home and opened the jar, it was rotten. I felt helpless because I knew I had to go back to exchange it and didn't know how to tell the clerk that something was wrong. I went back to the store, didn't say a word and just showed it to her.

My husband and I tried to learn English. For the first two years, we went to night school four days during the week, and on Saturdays we took another class at one of the local colleges. Our first teacher in night school was Paul Medeiros from Portugal. He was a wonderful teacher who did everything he could to help us learn. He would make gestures or drawings on the black board, and if that didn't work, he would get down on the floor and act things out. I admired him because he put his all into teaching.

I worked hard to keep my culture alive. At home we spoke Spanish. I made a list of proverbs, sayings and idioms we use back home so my kids would know what they meant. Also depending on the season, I would cook the things we cooked back in El Salvador, mostly everyday things like *chilate*, chocolate, *shuco* (a drink made from purple dried corn), *papusas*, cow feet soup, and beef stew. For Lent and Easter and every Friday we would eat fish done Salvadoran-style. The week before Easter Sunday, which is the week we paid most attention to, I made *tamales pisques,* which are tamales made with beans, and *torrejas*, which is like French toast with syrup. I would make all sorts of candies. For Christmas we would have a traditional turkey with tamales. I was teaching my kids to follow our traditions. It was like we were home.

> **My biggest worry was that my kids would fall into doing wrong things, like joining a gang or hanging out with kids who weren't good for them.**

My biggest worry was that my kids would fall into doing wrong things, like joining a gang or hanging out with kids who weren't good for them. I encouraged my kids to bring their friends home so I could know who they were. If they were home, they couldn't get into trouble. I think there is too much freedom for kids here. They can do anything and everything they want. They can even buy condoms and birth control. That would never happen back home. In our culture, we spend a lot of time with our children. And our kids don't leave when they're eighteen, as they do here. Even after they're married, the family continues to support and help them.

We also teach them to love, protect and respect their elders. That is something we never question. Here it seems that once people get older, they're put into a nursing home. This can happen in El Salvador, but only if the person is alone and doesn't have a family to take care of them. Otherwise, they live with their family. Families here seem more distant. People are more solitary. There are times I would like to be alone, but I always love to be with my family.

My Jobs in America

After I had been here for about a year or so, I found a job at a jewelry factory. My job was to place the earrings on a rack that would then be put into an oven to bake. I worked the night shift from 4 p.m. to midnight and made minimum wage, which at that time was $3.35 an hour. The factory was very cold and drafty, and most of the workers wore scarves, coats and hats to keep warm. We used lotion to wash our hands because there was no hot water. There were about 100 workers, mostly women, from South America, the Dominican Republic and Cuba; and even though we all spoke Spanish, the managers wouldn't allow us to talk with each other while we were working. They told us that we were there to work and not to talk.

After that job, I worked at a factory that made badges for the armed forces. My job was to place badges into a machine to be cut. In the summer they would put on the air conditioner, but in the winter they wouldn't put on the heater, so it was always cold. The hardest part of that job was that I had to stand the whole day. Before I got the job, I had fallen and twisted my ankle. I used my first paycheck to go to the doctor to make sure I didn't have a fracture because my ankle wouldn't heal. Every time I came home, my foot was huge because I was standing all day. I was paid minimum wage, about $110 a week. Then I got a 15-cent raise. The managers didn't like us to talk at that job either.

Teaching was work I loved and knew how to do. It had meaning. Here I was only working to subsidize my family.

After work, I would go home and prepare dinner, and then meet my husband at the college where we studied English until 9 p.m. We would get home an hour later because the school was far away. I was tired all the time.

The next job was working for a Cuban woman sewing borders around army emblems. This is where I learned how to sew. She treated us like family. We could talk together and celebrated all our birthdays. If you came in sick, she would give you medicine. We could listen to the radio.

I often daydreamed about teaching. I missed my work a lot. Teaching was work I loved and knew how to do. It had meaning. Here I was only working to subsidize my family. But then I would think about all the dangers and fear, and remember that at least here we didn't have that. I would just say, "I have to do this," and put my all into working hard and making a go of it, rather than dwelling on the past. I knew we had to finish what we started. The experience of leaving El Salvador and coming here has made me a stronger person. I'm not as innocent as I was. My heart and soul have hardened a bit. I understand politics better. I understand world problems better.

Juanita Continues Her Story

The day we left, all of our family came to say goodbye. We were crying. But it was also exciting because none of us had been on an airplane. I felt that we were on an adventure. It didn't hit me until later that we were leaving behind the life we knew. On the plane, my brother and mother were sitting next to a lady with long blond hair and a child with blue eyes and blond hair. This was our idea of a gringo. They were very friendly. My brother carried on a conversation with the boy in Spanish and the boy talked with my brother in English. They didn't understand each other, but they played and talked this way all the way to New York. On the layover in New Orleans, my brother and I discovered vending machines. My mom gave us quarters to buy candy. We didn't know English but we figured out how the machines worked and managed to buy a bunch of candy bars. This was our first experience with American junk food. My brother and I thought it was so cool. Chocolates, this is great.

My mom turned everything into an adventure. She made us try everything once to see if we liked it. She made things fun.

Life in America had different colors than our life in El Salvador. My memories from El Salvador are like a black-and-white picture, but here even in the darkest times there was always color. I felt safe here. I remember hanging out with my grandfather, which I had never done. He knew tons of stuff. He always wanted to go to the New York Public Library. Life was full of discoveries. But it was also hard. I missed my grandmothers. I missed the warm weather in El Salvador. I missed my house. I missed my room.

We went from having our own home to all four of us living in a small room in my aunt's house. It was hard living with my aunt. She has a strong personality. She is chaos. The weekends were the worst. Sometimes my aunt would ask us to leave the house if her friends were coming to visit, even in winter. Many times we would walk all day in the freezing cold before we could go back to our room. Although this was hard at first, in the long run it helped us. We became very familiar with the town we lived in, and this wouldn't have happened if we had not walked about during those long winter days.

I knew my mom missed my grandmother. She wrote tons of letters to her, and my father would make me write letters to his mother. Every time the news came on, we had to stay quiet so they could listen. Phone calls were precious. I knew they were expensive so they were few and far between. I never realized until we did these interviews how worried my mother was about her family. But we made the best of a bad situation, and the experience made us closer as a family. We had to rely on each other. We had nowhere else to turn.

The first place we lived there were mainly Latino people, mostly Cuban,

Dominicans and Peruvians, but also white people. We spent a lot of time at the Cuban bakery and butcher shop, and bought our fruits and vegetables at an Italian market. We bought Italian and Greek cheeses, which were similar to the cheeses in El Salvador. My mom turned everything into an adventure. She made us try everything once to see if we liked it. She made things fun. Her curiosity for new places and people transferred to us. We assimilated faster because we found that every culture has things that are similar.

I also discovered the telephone. Most people back home don't have a telephone. I called my cousins a lot but didn't realize there was a charge, so I got in some trouble. My cousins took me to different places like the malls. I was amazed that there was such an abundance of things here. I never saw that in El Salvador. Even though my parents weren't bad off financially, they didn't give us those kinds of luxuries. The other thing I remember is that I couldn't understand the concept of peanut butter and jelly. Why do you want to eat peanuts with jelly?

I started school at the end of the school year. They put me in the sixth grade, but told my family that I had the knowledge of a twelfth grader, which, of course, helped my self-esteem. My first teacher in the United States was Ms. Ertle. She was the nicest teacher ever. She asked me questions about El Salvador and shared my experiences with the other students. I felt she understood me.

I didn't know I was smart until I moved here. School was much easier for me here. In El Salvador I had homework every day, including weekends. I had to write a lot. I was doing research in third and fourth grade. In the United States, education is more relaxed. There is not as much pressure on the students to learn. People who become teachers in El Salvador really want to teach. Here many people fall into teaching by chance. There are a lot of wonderful teachers here, but there are some teachers who don't care.

At the beginning I didn't understand one thing my teacher said, and the students looked at me as if I was stupid because I couldn't say anything. I had to look everything up in the dictionary, and at times it was confusing because some words have more than one meaning. Other words I just didn't understand. One of the words that stumped me was acorn. Another was the word daddy. We never used daddy; we used father and papi. There was one student in my class, who spoke Spanish, and my teacher would communicate with me through her, but she was reluctant to speak Spanish with me. Maybe she was ashamed. Maybe she wanted to "be one of the kids" and leave Spanish at home. Some of the white kids were more open-minded than the Latino kids, which totally blew my mind.

I spent a lot of time just trying to make sense of the world around me because it was all in English. I felt like an alien. I didn't want to say something in fear that I would say it incorrectly. That was my biggest concern. My main goal was to learn English and get out of ESL (English as a Second Language) classes. I hated being in those classes. The teachers were great, but the other students looked down on you. When I finally got out, they put me into honors English. I

> *I was the spokesperson for the family. It made me realize that my mom was helpless, whereas before she had been an independent woman who didn't need me to speak for her.*

had learned English in three months, and after a year and a half, I was thinking in English. But my mom kept on us to keep practicing Spanish so we wouldn't lose it, but I did lose some.

The kids here were more sophisticated than the kids in El Salvador. We were more sheltered and innocent. We lived for recess and colored pencils, and stickers were a big deal. Here the girls were interested in boys and trying out make-up and new hair styles. I didn't get into that until I was in the ninth grade. My dad was super-overprotective. He wouldn't even let me go to a baseball game or a movie at night. Even after I got my California driver's license, he wouldn't let me drive. He didn't think I was ready. My mom gave me a little more freedom.

I sensed a change in my mother. In El Salvador, she was always working until late at night on lessons and projects for her students. She was the kind of teacher who was always trying to find new things to do with her kids. She was also used to living in her own home and doing things she wanted. Everything was different for her here. Our relationship also changed. In El Salvador I relied solely on my mother because she knew the lay of the land. Here neither of us knew the lay of the land, but I knew English so I would be the one that would talk for her. I was the one that asked for directions, or how to fill things out. I was the spokesperson for the family. It made me realize that my mom was helpless, whereas before she had been an independent woman who didn't need me to speak for her. That's difficult for a kid. The movie Spanglish makes this point. In the movie, the mother asks her daughter to translate what she is saying. The daughter is embarrassed, but she has to do what her mother asks her to do. You have an inner struggle. On the one hand, you don't want to translate certain things because you're embarrassed, but on the other hand, you know that if you don't, you'll be in trouble. You just want the earth to open up and swallow you, especially when you're a teenager.

By the ninth grade I was pretty much assimilated. I attended the High School for the Performing Arts, where I studied music. I played the flute. It was great because the music students were more open-minded. They were curious about me. There was only one kid from El Salvador in my class. He had moved here when he was thirteen and was having a hard time relating to the American experience. He liked to talk with me about what he missed about El Salvador. Then I met someone from Honduras who was excited because he could speak Spanish with me the way he did at home.

Ana Continues Her Story

My Family Moves to Los Angeles

On July 5, 1987, my family moved to Los Angeles. It was a hard decision because my husband was making good money in New Jersey, but I thought the weather would be better for Juanita, and I had more family here than in New Jersey. By that time, my mother and siblings were all living in Los Angeles. The only one who didn't want to move was Juanita. She cried all the time.

We moved in with one of my brothers. Once again we were living with family, but this time it was better. My brothers and I had at least grown up together. After three months, we moved to a house across the street from my brother, and we have not moved again. The owner of the house rented it to us despite the fact that there were seven of us living in that small house: the four of us, my younger sister, my mother and stepfather. It was great living with my mom, and the climate was perfect.

Everything was easier in Los Angeles. By this time, I had become accustomed to this country. My husband had a hard time finding a job, but I was luckier and after a month, my sister and I found jobs at an electronics company. I worked for the company for

I think that diversity is one of the greatest things about this country. It's beautiful.

over sixteen years and was promoted several times. This was my best job in the United States. The owner of the company was a good man, a humanitarian who liked it when his workers moved forward in life. He paid for his workers to go to college and offered free English classes three days a week after work.

The owner took pride in the fact that it was an international company. There were people from Russia, Italy, Armenia, China, Vietnam, Japan, England, and many from Mexico, El Salvador and Guatemala. This is how I learned English. Everyone had to try and speak English, even if it was bad English, in order to communicate. We had parties all the time. Everyone would bring food from their culture to share. I think that diversity is one of the greatest things about this country. It's beautiful.

When the owner died, his brother-in-law took over, but he was a different kind of boss. He only cared about production and profits, and quickly got rid of the old employees so he could hire new people for less money. I was one of the people he got rid of. Because of the repetitive nature of my work, I had developed tendonitis in my elbow. When I asked him to provide me with a table to rest my arm on, he fired me.

Ana's Reflections

I fell in love with this country for greeting me with open arms, and I have never regretted my decision to leave El Salvador and come here. This country has given us stability. I would like Americans to know that as an immigrant I came here to work and get ahead, and thankfully we have incorporated ourselves into the society. I love the fact that I can say what I want here. I can complain and fight for my rights, and I don't have to do that in a nasty way. I can be polite. I am grateful to this country because it has given me a lot. It has given my children education, which could not have happened in El Salvador. Also, there are many more services for disabled people. The school here told us that if Juanita didn't have transportation to get to school, they would pick her up and take her, and if she couldn't go to school because of her disability, they would send a teacher to teach her. This would not have happened in El Salvador. There, services for people with disabilities are only for millionaires.

There, services for people with disabilities are only for millionaires.

But even though I have lived here for twenty-six years and have become accustomed to this country, I identify as a Salvadoran woman, and I was very happy that I could have dual citizenship. My roots are in El Salvador—the folklore, history, customs, and environment. When I'm in El Salvador, I feel comfortable and happy. I feel that I am where I should be. I feel welcome. Also the pace of living is less hectic than here. Life goes by slower. It's less stressful. But at the same time everything in El Salvador is completely different. I don't know too many people. My friends are gone. My husband and I are getting older and it is harder for us to get around. The streets have bumps which make it easy to fall, there are no elevators or handicapped ramps, and the buses don't wait for you. It is more convenient living here. Services to the public are much better.

My country is suffering from the effects of the Civil War. The hope was that things would get better, but they have only gotten worse. Many people died and it seems they died for nothing. Many well-educated people—lawyers, engineers, business administrators—cannot find jobs. You have to know someone to get a job today. I think we've gone backwards.

Juanita Continues Her Story

I moved to Los Angeles when I was seventeen, two weeks after I graduated from high school. I didn't want to move because I had finally made friends, and was making plans about college. I cried a lot. Moving to Los Angeles meant starting over again. But it was a lot easier this time because I already knew

English. Another thing that helped was that we were able to get our own home about two months after we got here, and we didn't have to live with relatives for too long a period of time. And the weather was not as crazy.

It turned out that the move to Los Angeles was the best thing that could have happened to me. The move made me more independent. I learned how to get around by bus, I got a job, and despite the fact that my dad tried to keep me on a short leash, I went out with friends. In the fall of 1988, I enrolled in Los Angeles City College. I became friends with a woman from El Salvador named Ana who opened my mind to politics, but it wasn't until I enrolled at the University of Southern California that I was ready to talk about the Civil War in El Salvador. The memories had been buried so deep inside of me, that I couldn't touch them. That changed when I took a class on Central and South American politics.

University of Southern California graduation, 2001. Juanita is third from the left.

One day my professor told us that he was going to show a documentary about the Civil War in El Salvador. I knew he was planning on showing the documentary, but what I didn't know was that he was planning to show it that day. It took me by complete surprise. The film was old and blurry; everything was in black and white. When the film started to roll, I realized that I had seen the images before. I had lived through that. It hit me like a ton of bricks. There was footage of people getting shot, and footage of the nuns who were killed. There was footage of the guerillas taking over the cathedral. There was footage of burning buildings. There was footage of a violent protest where a lot of people got killed. You could see how enraged the government was at the people for helping the guerillas. I thought— they're filming these people. Some of the people weren't wearing masks. The government will know who they are. Those people are probably dead.

I was completely petrified. Everything from my childhood came back. I remembered my fear when my parents went out, fear that I might not see them again. My mom might not pick me up at school. My dad might not come home from work. My school might be destroyed. My friends might be killed. I could be killed. Before the war, we led pretty simple lives. My childhood was happy and innocent. I felt protected. The people in El Salvador were innocent, and that got

People here don't know what it's like to live with that kind of fear.

destroyed with all the bombs. It shatters your psyche. All of that stays with you. People here don't know what it's like to live with that kind of fear.

When the documentary ended, my professor asked me to talk about my experiences, but at first I couldn't. I had closed this off in my mind when I came to the United States, but then the students began talking about what they had seen. One student said that he was tired of learning about "these" wars, and another student said that in "those countries when you light a cigarette, everything catches on fire." Then when I couldn't hold back anymore, I told the students that their careless analysis really pissed me off. I told them that I had lived through this. I had seen it happen.

This class motivated me to study foreign policy and learn about other cultures. I wanted to help bring the world together. In 2001, I received my Bachelor's degree in International Relations and Spanish. I picked Spanish because I have always been interested in literature and writing. I had an immense fear of writing in English, but I am an excellent writer in Spanish. Spanish has helped me become more involved in my own culture and the Latino culture at large.

For the past several years, I have worked as a paralegal at a community law office called Working People's Law Center near downtown Los Angeles. I do this job because I like helping people move forward with their lives, although the odds are sometimes stacked against them. But my goal is to become a writer and tell stories from my life. I have so many stories to tell.

I live in the back of my parent's house, literally a stone's throw away from their front door, in a mostly Salvadoran neighborhood where even the dog speaks

Spanish; and my brother, his wife and new baby live next door. I visit my parents for breakfast, lunch and dinner and then go home; and my brother begins each day checking in on them. Even though my brother and I are grown, my parents continue to look out for us. When I am out of the house with friends or I am running late getting home, my father still calls me several times a

Salvadora (left) and Rita in the house in El Salvador, 1982.

day to make sure I'm all right. My mom is one of my best friends. We talk about everything. That's my culture. My parents took care of my grandparents until they died, and my brother and I feel the same sense of responsibility to our parents. We want to help them as much as we can. We kid around about putting them in a nursing home, but we never would. Nursing homes are horrible places Recently, one of my grandmothers died. She lived with us for many years and was a vital part of our family. She loved telling me stories about her life. She was our history. For us, family is everything.

Juanita's Reflections

For a long time I didn't know where I belonged. I didn't belong here, and I didn't belong in El Salvador. Now I am comfortable in my own skin. I am part of El Salvador and I am part of this country, but it's a precarious balance, one that has to be maintained with care and precision. The Salvadoran part of me is very strong. I believe that it's important to keep close to your culture. It will help you figure out who you are. I am Salvadoran at home with my parents and other relatives, and when people are visiting. That is because I have to interact with them in Spanish and the whole Salvadoran side just spills out. I am Salvadoran when I drive because I am constantly fighting with other drivers in Spanish the way my dad does, and to me that is Salvadoran.

I'm also happy to be an American. Here in the United States I have the freedom not to get married. In El Salvador, I would have definitely been married by now, probably with a lot of problems. There aren't many men like my dad who are comfortable in their own skin, and who are supportive of a strong woman. Here I can also criticize the government without fear. I can read whatever I want without fear. I can talk about things without fear. I can discuss politics without fear. I don't have to burn my books. I don't have a fear that if our neighbor hears something, he'll tell the death squads and the death squad will come and take us away in the middle of the night.

Also important to me is that here I can have a car, which would have never happened in El Salvador. Such things are only accessible to millionaires. I have a friend who grew up with me in El Salvador who has cerebral palsy. He is a smart kid, really active, but he can't move around easily because he can't drive. Without a car, it's hard for him to be independent. Everybody points out that he is disabled. They pity him. Here, I am able to forget that I am disabled. I have always hated people who pity me. There is nothing to pity.

I've grown up and gone to school here in the United States. I've been in-volved in the culture here. I have become attached to this country. This is my home. From my point of view, this is truly the country of opportunities. If you want to make something of yourself, you can do it. If you're positive and want to move forward, you can. There are no limits.

María's and Michelle's Stories

María Luisa Onody was born on June 21, 1960, in the state of Durango in central Mexico. When she was four years old, her father, Catarino Sarinana, left their home for the first time and began traveling to the United States in search of better job opportunities. Catarino continued making this trip every year for the next forty-one years, stopping only in 2007 at the age of seventy for health reasons. María joined her father in Los Angeles for the first time when she was ten years old and, like her father, continued making this journey many more times. María currently lives in Los Angeles with her husband, Laszlo, and her two daughters, Fiorela and Michelle Garcia who, like their mother and grandfather, spent much of their childhoods traveling back and forth between Durango and Los Angeles. Here are María's and Michelle's stories.

María

Michelle

Historical Note:
Mexican people were living in the western and southern parts of North America well before the United States existed. Until the signing of the Treaty of Guadalupe Hidalgo at the conclusion of the Mexican American War (1846-1848), a large part of the southwest belonged to Mexico, including the land that would become California and Texas, along with parts of Colorado, New Mexico, Utah and Nevada. The treaty gave this land to the United States in exchange for $15 million dollars. Shortly after, the United States purchased what is now southern Arizona and New Mexico for $10 million. This is known as the Gadsden Purchase.

Over the past century, Mexican immigration has ebbed and flowed, depending for the most part on the economic needs of the United States and Mexico. Both countries benefit from immigrant labor. United States' employers often exploit Mexican workers paying low wages without benefits, and the Mexican economy prospers from the money that workers send back home. According to Mexico's Central Bank, the Mexican economy took in $23.9 billion in 2007 in so-called *"remittances," money that workers send back to support their families. These payments altogether are Mexico's second largest source of revenue after petroleum.*

The first significant wave of immigration came during and after the Mexican Revolution of 1910. A strong economy in the United States and the violence of the Revolution drove thousands of Mexicans to the United States. Between 1910 and 1930, the number of immigrants from Mexico tripled, going from 200,000 to 600,000. During World War II, there was once again a need for workers, especially farm workers. This resulted in the establishment of the "bracero program," which allowed millions of Mexican men to come to the United States to work on short-term labor contracts. Approximately 4.5 million Mexican workers came to work under this program, which lasted from 1942 to 1964.

Today, there are approximately 20 million people of Mexican origin living in the United States. More than 25 percent of all Mexican immigrants have come since 2000. Most are men of working age who, like those who preceded them, come to find work to support their families back home. A news article in the San Diego Union Tribune *dated July 5, 2007, noted that 47 percent of Mexico's population suffers from poverty at various levels depending on the region, with 18.2 percent living in "extreme poverty," defined as too poor to buy sufficient food. In his September 2007 State of the Union Address, Mexican President Felipe Calderón blamed the people's plight on the Mexican government for failing to build an economy that offers all of its people good jobs and a decent education.*

María Begins Her Story

My Grandparents

My grandfather (my mother's father), Pascual Espinoza, was born in the state of Zacatecas in central Mexico in 1912. He started working in the fields when he was five or six years old and never went to school or learned how to read or write. My grandparents were very poor, and in those times it was common for young children to go to work to help the family. My grandfather worked as a migrant worker until he was sixty years old, and when he could no longer do this work, he and my grandmother, Nicanora Debora, started a small business selling candies to make ends meet. My grandfather was a very happy and funny man who loved to tell jokes and dance. I remember that he would put on different kinds of music like *rancheras* (cowboy songs), and the family would all dance around the room.

Nicanora Debora, my grandmother, was born in Zacatecas around 1917. I think she went to elementary school because she once told me that she had a *pizarrón* (blackboard) in her home. She and my grandfather had fifteen children together, but only five survived. My memory of my grandmother is that she was always at home taking care of the children and the house. My grandparents lived on a small ranch outside the city of Zacatecas, and when I was a child, we often visited them. It was a very peaceful place with lots of different animals, like chickens, pigs and donkeys. My grandfather loved taking us around town on his donkeys. I especially liked spending Easter with my grandparents. They always prepared a special dinner of gorditas with chili, beans and cheese inside; traditional desserts; and red, yellow and green tortillas.

My grandparents and their children traveled two or three times a year from Zacatecas to Durango, which is north of Zacatecas, to work in the fields. They picked cotton in Durango, grapes in another city, tomatoes in another. When they began traveling, they didn't have cars or buses, so the whole family walked from city to city with their donkey. My grandfather would tell me, "I get lost when I take the bus." During vacations from school, I often spent time with them. It was so calm. I remember we all stayed in one small room with a tiny kitchen and a chimney. There was no light and no bathroom, and we all slept together on the concrete floor. I loved that.

My other grandfather (my father's father), Catarino Sarinana Pereira, was born in Durango, Mexico, around 1917. He was an unhappy and distant man. Neither my father nor I had a close relationship with him. My father's mother, Agustina Ledezma, was born in Texas, United States, but I don't know when she was born or what part of Texas she was from. I don't know anything about her life because she died when my father was a few months old.

My Parents

My mother, Hortencia Sarinana, was born in Zacatecas, Mexico, in 1939. She was one of five children. She had one sister and three brothers. Her father (my grandfather) sent her to school, but she only went for a short time because she didn't like school. She never learned how to read or write, and I think that later in life she regretted this. When she was a child, she was a tomboy who preferred to stay outside and climb trees instead of going to school. Her parents were very strict with her. She couldn't leave the house or wear make-up. She wanted to cut her hair, but her parents wouldn't let her do that either.

Historical Note:
The name Zacatecas *belongs to the indigenous people who lived there before the Spanish came in the 1500s. The Spanish took over the city and transported Zacatecas' silver all over the world. Mining is no longer important. Tourism is now the primary industry in this city of over 122,889 people. Zacatecas is a beautiful city with many elaborate colonial buildings and fountains.*

My mother started working in the fields when she was seven years old and spent the rest of her childhood traveling with her family from city to city to work.

My mother started working in the fields when she was seven years old and spent the rest of her childhood traveling with her family from city to city to work. She didn't like this work, but she had no choice. Like many other children at that time, she had to help her family. It is still common to see children as young as eight working in the fields. Working in the fields was hard. She was afraid of snakes, and when she wasn't working hard enough, people would hit her or pull her braids. My mother never wanted me to work in the fields as she did. She wanted me to be able to go out with my friends to dances and parties. She couldn't do this when she was young and wanted me to have these experiences, but I have always been shy and reserved. I never wanted that kind of life.

My father, Catarino Sarinana, was born in Durango, Mexico, in 1937. When his mother died, his father remarried. My father was raised by his stepmother, who never had any children of her own. She loved my father, but I never heard my father call her "Mother." I really don't know very much about my father's early life because while I was growing up, he was always in Los Angeles working, but I don't think he had a very happy childhood. He always wanted a better life for his children. He wanted his children to go to school and have more opportunities than he did.

My parents got married when my mother was fifteen and my father was seventeen. By this time my mother was working as a housekeeper, and one day as she was walking home from work, she met my father. They started talking and eventually fell in love and moved in together. One day after they were living together, my father came home from work, grabbed my mother and told her they were going to church to get married. That day all marriages were free. My mother was in her apron washing dishes at the time, so she didn't even

Maria's father, Catarino Sarinana, seventeen years old, 1955.

Historical Note:

Durango is one of Mexico's largest states yet has the second-lowest population density—approximately 1,509,117 in the 2005 census. The state is heavily mountainous with an arid climate. Nevertheless, it has a rich agricultural area and is the second largest producer of goat's milk. It is also the state's primary producer of pine and oak trees. In the 1970s it became a major producer of wood products and is the home of Latin America's largest paper company.

Durango is famous for its scorpions. Mexicans often refer to someone from Durango as Alacrán de Durango *(a scorpion from Durango). Francisco (Pancho) Villa is the state's most famous son, having made a lasting mark in Mexican history for his actions during the Mexican Revolution.*

Cattle ranching, agriculture and mining continue to be major industries although these have suffered since the mid-twentieth century, and a general lack of economic opportunity is apparent. Like its neighboring state Zacatecas, Durango has one of Mexico's highest levels of emigration.

have time to get ready. I'm pretty sure that my mom wanted a big wedding because she always loved parties, but they didn't have enough money for that. My parents have been married for over fifty years.

My mom had eleven children, five boys and six girls, but three died shortly after they were born. She had a baby every two years. The oldest is my brother Catarino, followed by Margarito who died, me, my sisters Agustina, Ofelia, Lupita, and Ramona (also known as Monis), my brother Gerardo, who died while we were living in Los Angeles, my brother Gerardo, who was named after my brother who died, Alma Rosa, and Juan, who also died. As the oldest daughter, I was responsible for taking care of my younger sisters and brothers and helping my mother with all the housework. In my culture, the oldest daughter is like a second mom, and the oldest son helps the family financially. I never resented that. This was a normal part of life. I was happy growing

María's mother, Hortencia, in her early twenties in Durango, 1957.

92

We knew everyone in the neighborhood and everyone knew us. Everybody watched out for the children. We always felt safe.

up. The only thing I didn't like was when my mom would leave me alone with one of the babies. I remember once when I was in fifth grade, my mother asked me to cook dinner because she was busy washing all the clothes. I did a horrible job and she was very angry at me. My father pretended to like what I cooked. My mother was always very strict with me and got mad at me for everything. Maybe she was strict with me because her parents were the same way with her. My father was different. He always protected me.

I grew up in a small city in the state of Durango called Gómez Palacio, which is an industrial city with a lot of factories, including a soap factory where many people in the city work. When I was five years old, my parents moved from a house on the outskirts of the city to one closer to the downtown area. In Mexico most people own their own homes. There are not a lot of apartments like here. The house was pink and pistachio green. My father must have loved those colors because he's painted every house he's owned with the same ones. He also loves green mosaic tiles because he also has them in all of his houses. Our

> *Historical Note:*
> *Gómez Palacio is a city of about 240,000 people located in the eastern part of the state of Durango. Founded on September 15, 1885, the city is named for Francisco Gómez Palacio y Bravo, a writer and politician.*

house had three small bedrooms, all painted yellow, one for my parents, and one for my oldest brother and the third for all the girls. Mornings were always my favorite time. I loved being at the table with food and all the family. Sometimes there were so many people eating breakfast that the children had to sit on the floor to eat.

Growing up, I always knew that we were poor. We didn't have many clothes or shoes and sometimes we had to go to the pawn shop when we didn't have any money. This wasn't unusual; most people in our community were struggling to get by, and there were many people worse off than we were. It never bothered me that we were poor. We enjoyed what we had. We were a close community. We knew everyone in the neighborhood and everyone knew us. Everybody watched out for the children. We always felt safe. Even when families move, which isn't too often, there is always someone who stays, so you never lose track of anyone. It's different here. People move around a lot. Nobody knows your history. Nobody knows anything about you.

I loved school and always got good grades, but my mother never encouraged me to go further than elementary school. She didn't think women needed an education because their role in life was to get married and take care of their children and home. It was different for men. They needed an education because they had to support their family. It's funny because out of all my brothers and sisters, I was the only one who wanted to go further in school, and because I was a girl, I couldn't. My father had different ideas. He wanted all of us to have an education. He always loved to read and learn, but he wasn't able to complete school because when he was young, he had to work to help support the family. But after he and my mom got married, he went back to school to finish elementary school. It was a common practice at that time in Mexico for people to complete school when they were adults.

I completed primary and secondary school. I wanted to go to preparatory school to continue my studies, but

In Durango, 1966. Caterino at top, María, Agustina, and Ofelia.

I knew that this would be hard on my family because preparatory school cost a lot of money. The decision was taken out of my hands. When I was sixteen, we went to Los Angeles to live for two months, and when I returned to Mexico I had missed registration for preparatory school. My only option was to enroll in Escuela Normal, which prepares you to become a teacher. I was disappointed. I wanted to become someone important like a lawyer. Teaching wasn't my dream.

My father started coming to the United States to work in 1964 when I was about four years old and continued doing this every year while I was growing up. Sometimes he would stay seven or eight months, other times just a few months, and he never went at the same time of the year. We knew he was getting ready to leave when we saw him packing his suitcase. When he left, he would tell us, "Be good." We all cried. It was hard on all of us. My parents never sat us down to explain why he was leaving. Parents didn't explain these things to children.

My mother never wanted my father to go to the United States, which she still brings up to him. It was hard on her. She didn't have anyone to confide in, and she couldn't call him because we didn't have a telephone. I wrote letters for my mother because she never learned how to read or write, but my father didn't always answer her right away. Sometimes my father couldn't send money home. I remember hearing stories in the neighborhood about husbands who would leave

Top: Catarino.
Middle: María,
Lupita,
Hortencia,
Monis, Agustina.
Bottom: Ofelia,
1970.

Mexico, find another wife and family, and stop sending money back home. I remember feeling scared whenever I would see my mother smoking because I had a feeling that meant we were having financial problems. Now I understand how much pressure she was under, but at the time I didn't understand why she was moody and always yelling.

When we were out of money, I would go to the pawn shop to sell things like blenders, toasters, and one time, my dad's guitar. My mother had a line of credit at the local corner store, which was a common practice in our community, so when my father couldn't send money, she could buy groceries on credit. Sometimes my mother sold candies, sodas and cookies out of our house to make a little extra money. These little businesses were pretty common in the community. Women would bring in a little money for groceries or shoes by selling things out of their homes, like ice cream, beans, covers for notebooks and hair bows.

Most of the time, my father worked in Beverly Hills as a tailor in large department stores like Neiman Marcus and Nordstrom. He had been trained to be a tailor in Mexico and owned a tailor shop near our home, but he felt he had to go to Los Angeles because he earned more money there. Many times my father would tell us, "This will be the last time." But we needed the money, and once you start coming here, it's hard to stop. You have to understand that people in Mexico are poor. They don't have the things we have here. My father wanted us to have a better life. I think if he had not come to the United States to work and had stayed in Mexico, probably he wouldn't have been able to buy his family a house or send his children to school.

My father tried to make up for being gone so much of the time by bringing back as many appliances as he could. I remember that he brought back an industrial sewing machine, and a radio, television set and VCR. The ladies in the neighborhood would come to our house at night to watch *novelas* (soap operas) on

95

our television set, and the kids would come during the day to watch cartoons. The only thing he couldn't bring back was a stove. He couldn't fit it on his lap. He continued doing that every time he went away.

He never expressed how sad he was that he missed so many things in his children's lives. He kept things inside.

My father missed out on a lot. He was home for most of the holidays, like Easter and Christmas, but he often missed our birthdays because there were so many of us. He never expressed how sad he was that he missed so many things in his children's lives. He kept things inside. When I turned fifteen, my father was in Los Angeles. In Mexico when girls turn fifteen they have their *quinceañera,* which is an important tradition—the day a girl becomes a woman. Girls wait their whole lives for this day. I wanted my father to be with me so I waited one year until I was sixteen to have my party. We didn't have a big party, just dinner and a few friends, but I felt it was important that my father be with me on that day.

My First Trip to the United States

The first time I came to the United States, I was ten years old. I guess you could say that I was following a family tradition that began when my grandparents began traveling back and forth from Zacatecas to Durango to work in the fields. My father continued that tradition when he began traveling back and forth from Mexico to Los Angeles for work. Then when my mother became tired of this, she told my father that he had to take the family with him, so we all joined him on the bus. I am pretty sure that one of the reasons I got married was that I didn't want to travel anymore. I wanted to end this tradition.

Coming to the United States was a big adventure, and we were all really excited. We came by bus, which takes twenty-four hours, and I remember feeling

Durango, 1976. Top: Agustina, María, Ofelia; Middle: Lupita, Hortencia, Monis; Bottom: Gerardo, Alma Rosa.

really scared because the roads on the Sierra Madre are very windy and narrow. We had permits to cross the border, but only for a few days, so we could only bring a few suitcases for the whole family. I remember that I took three changes of clothes, the best ones I had. We moved into an apartment near MacArthur Park where my father had been living. Everything was big and scary at the same time.

Most of the time, we stayed in the apartment because my mother didn't want us to go outside. Maybe she was worried about our immigration status. Once when we were playing outside the building, someone told my mother that we had done something bad. My mother got very mad and spanked us, even though we hadn't done anything wrong. She never asked us what had happened. We were all obedient and did whatever our parents said.

We only stayed a few months in Los Angeles. I remember that there was an earthquake. My mother was pregnant at this time, and after the earthquake she lost the baby. Later, my father had to go to the hospital because he was bleeding out of his nose. The doctors said that he was okay, but when he came home the bleeding started again, and my father decided to go back to Mexico. I think if we had stayed in the United States that time, my future would have been different. I'm pretty sure that I would have done something with my life. I would have gone to school. I would have finished my studies here.

When I was twenty-one, I graduated from Escuela Normal. There were so many teachers who graduated that year that it was difficult to find a job. The only teaching jobs available were in the hills outside the city, and my father wouldn't let me go because he felt that the area was too dangerous. The people who lived there were mostly uneducated, and they carried knives and machetes. Besides, in Mexico, girls don't move out of the home until they are married. It's not like here where kids leave home at eighteen and live on their own. I ended up finding a job in the city as a cashier. Looking back, I should have tried to convince my parents to let me work as a teacher. My life would have been very different. I would have definitely gone further with my education. But it was impossible. I always believed everything my parents said was correct, the right thing. This is my culture.

In 1980 when I was twenty, my father told us that we were going back to Los Angeles to work. I didn't want to go, but I had no choice. So I went.

María at twenty, 1980.

My father and one of my brothers went to Los Angeles; and two of my sisters, my brother's family and I went to Bakersfield because there was no place to live in Los Angeles. My mother and four sisters stayed in Mexico. My mother didn't like living in the United States because she felt that it was too dangerous. Mexico was her home. She felt safe there. While I was in Bakersfield, I stayed with my father's *compadre* (the person who baptizes your child, now used to describe a close friend) for two months and worked in the fields picking grapes. Every day we woke up at 4 a.m. and started work at 5 a.m. I knew this was only temporary until we moved back to Los Angeles to start again, but I liked the feeling of working hard during the day and being really hungry at lunch.

We only had what we absolutely needed. Just the basics. We never had enough of anything.

When I returned to Los Angeles, my family moved from apartment to apartment to apartment, from job to job to job. Things are a blur. It was crazy. I had several different jobs in downtown Los Angeles. One time I sold magazines, another time jeans, and another time knickknacks. During this time we went back and forth to Mexico at least three different times. We always kept our clothes in Mexico and took whatever we could in our suitcase. When we were here, we used whatever clothes we could get. Sometimes my family would give us clothes to wear. We only had what we absolutely needed. Just the basics. We never had enough of anything. But we never planned to live here; we were just here to work and go back to Mexico.

When I was about twenty-four, I decided to stay in Los Angeles. I was tired of all the traveling around. I felt disconnected.

When I was about twenty-four, I decided to stay in Los Angeles. I was tired of all the traveling around. I felt disconnected. I just wanted to be stable and live in one place, and I thought that there would be more opportunities for a better life here than in Mexico. I knew that if I stayed here, I would need to learn English. Nobody in my family had learned English. My parents didn't think there was any reason since we were only here to work and would always return to Mexico to live.

I enrolled in adult school with three of my sisters. It was funny. When the four of us would come to class, the teacher would always say, "The whole family came to class." This is where I met my future husband Andrés, who was twenty-nine and still single. At least that's what he told me. He told me that he had not met the right girl because he had been traveling back and forth to Mexico so much. But then I found out from his neighbor that he was married and that his wife was living in Mexico. I told him we were finished, but he kept insisting and insisting, and since I was in love with him, I agreed to get married. I knew we couldn't be married in a church because he was already married. I was afraid to tell my father, but I knew I had to. He was very angry at me and wanted to send me back to Mexico. He told me that I had disappointed him. This was the first time I had gone against my parents' wishes. We got married in the courthouse in 1985. None of my family came to my wedding.

I got pregnant right away. My oldest daughter, Fiorela, was born on February 27, 1987, and my second daughter, Michelle, was born a year later on May 9. My husband and I argued a lot. Two of his nephews came to live with us, and even though they worked, they didn't help out financially. Also my husband had to help his family in Mexico. After our last fight, he stopped talking to me. I told him we should try to work things out, but he didn't want to, and after five years of marriage, he moved out. After he left, the only thing I could do was to move back to Mexico to live with my parents. I felt it was impossible to raise my two daughters alone, and I knew that my parents would never allow me to live on my own with my daughters. This is my culture. Family takes care of each other. Nobody lives alone.

In San Pedro, 1991. Michelle, María, cousin Alicia, and Fiorela.

Life was very difficult for me in Mexico. We didn't have any money, and I couldn't work because I had to take care of my daughters who were two and three years old. I wanted them to go to kindergarten, but in Mexico families have to pay for kindergarten, and I didn't have the money. I knew my daughters could go to kindergarten for free here, so a year or so after moving to Mexico, we moved back to the United States to live with my sister Ofelia's family in San Pedro, which is south of downtown Los Angeles. We stayed with my sister for two years and then moved back to Mexico to live with my parents. Every time my parents would come, they would push me to come back with them to Mexico. They thought it would be better for the kids.

After about two years in San Pedro, we moved back to Mexico. We stayed about a year and then moved back to the United States again. We moved in with my sister Ofelia and her family who had moved to Los Angeles, and my daughters went to the local elementary school. In 1999 when Michelle was eleven and Fiorela was twelve, we moved back to Mexico again. My daughters were happy in Mexico. They loved being around family. But I couldn't work because I had to stay home and take care of the kids. My mother couldn't help because she had high blood pressure. I didn't think I could make it financially. I was spending the money I had brought with me too fast. Also I saw that it wasn't good for my daughters to have so many changes in their lives, and that if we continued this way, going back and forth and back and forth all the time, they would never learn English, and I knew that if they didn't learn English, they would never succeed. So after six or seven months in Mexico, I decided we needed to move back to the United States, but this time for good. I felt bad. My daughters cried a lot. They wanted to stay in Mexico. But I felt I had no choice but to come back. I wanted a better life for my daughters, and I thought there were more opportunities in the United States. If we had stayed in Mexico, I don't know if they would have gone to college. Probably they would be working in low-paying jobs.

This time, we moved to the city of Rosemead, where my sister Ofelia, her husband and two children were now living. We stayed there for a year and a half and then moved back to Los Angeles to live with my parents. My father never stopped coming here to work, but at some point my mother started to come with him even though she felt her home was in Mexico and never liked living here. This time when my parents returned to Mexico, my daughters and I didn't go back with them. We stayed in the apartment in Los Angeles. This was the first time I had lived alone with my two daughters. I was forty-one; Michelle was thirteen and Fiorela was fourteen. I was scared. I had always done what my parents said. I didn't know if I could work and take care of everything, but I thought, "I have to do this." My daughters were older and it was time that we

started to do our own thing. Living in my parents' house meant following their rules, and living in my sisters' houses meant following their rules. Living alone with my daughters meant that I could set my own rules. For the first time in my life, I felt that I could do anything I wanted to do. I felt free. I felt independent. I was able to do what I wanted without anyone telling me what to do. I loved that. I especially loved spending weekends with my daughters.

I found a job at a small store in the neighborhood

Michelle, sister Fiorela, and María.
Michelle is four years old.

I had to ask my daughters to translate for me, which I didn't like. As a mom, it is my job to speak for them and to defend them. . . Not knowing English has made me feel frustrated and impotent.

doing just about everything and anything they wanted me to do. Sometimes I was the cashier; other times I shelved merchandise or worked the floor. I worked seven or eight hours a day, six days a week, and then would go home and clean the house, cook and take care of my daughters. I was happy. But it was hard to raise two daughters alone, especially without a car and language. Language has been the hardest thing about living here. I hated the fact that I couldn't help my daughters in school, and I felt embarrassed because I couldn't talk with their teachers. I had to ask my daughters to translate for me, which I didn't like. As a mom, it is my job to speak for them and to defend them. This was backwards. It was very uncomfortable for me. Not knowing English has made me feel frustrated and impotent.

I also worried about my daughters all the time. I was working long hours, and most of the time I couldn't be with them when they came home from school. My biggest worry was that my daughters would become like other American girls. They wanted to become more Americanized to fit in, which is natural, but I was scared when I saw young girls skipping school and hanging out on the streets with their friends and boyfriends. I was scared about the dangers outside and the people who could influence them. Kids here have too much freedom. Both parents work and there isn't anyone at home after school to take care of the kids. Everybody does what they want. My daughters and I fought a lot. I wanted them to respect the things that I taught them, like listening to their parents and obeying the rules of the house, the same values my mother taught me. My daughters wanted more freedom. It was very difficult.

My Second Husband

For many years, my daughters were the people who gave me the strength to keep fighting. I never thought I would get married again. I had decided to raise my daughters alone and then maybe when my daughters were older and out of the house, then I might meet someone and maybe get married. But I thought that by that time, I would be too old. Then a few years ago a friend from church introduced me to a man named Laszlo, who was from Hungary. At first I thought we would just be friends. I always felt I would be with someone from my own country who shared the same culture, but then as we got to know each other and

I felt comfortable with him, that didn't matter. Laszlo turned out to be the man of my dreams. My family never cared that he was from another culture. They thought I had the right to be happy. In the beginning, my daughters had a hard time accepting Laszlo, which I thought was natural because they had never seen me with a man, but I knew that with time they would grow to like him because he was a good man. But I also told them that if they had any problems with Laszlo, I would leave him and things would go back to the way they were before. Laszlo and I lived together for two years and then we got married.

María's Reflections

I consider myself a Mexican because I was born in Mexico and my parents raised me with certain customs and values, like respecting what parents say. But the more time I spend here, the more American I feel. This is natural. With experience comes change. When I was growing up, I thought that my role in life was to get married and take care of my family and home. I no longer think that a woman should get married just because that is what is expected of her. When I was growing up, my parents would not let me out of the house to study or travel without being married. When I see my daughters going to the university and participating in the community, I think back and realize that I didn't have those opportunities. My mother didn't give me that freedom. My mother didn't let me be who I am. I'm trying to be different with my daughters. I want them to be who they want to be. I do believe in love and would like my daughters to find someone who loves and respects them for who they are; but if they don't, my daughters

Six sisters at reunion in Durango, 1998. María is top right.

will still have their education and careers. My mother wouldn't agree. She would probably say: "I don't know why you think like that. That is not the way I raised you. That is not what I taught you."

Michelle's Story

The first time I went to Mexico I was two years old and my sister was three, but my first memories were when I was four. I came two times that year, the first time around my fourth birthday, and the other to celebrate posada *at my grandmother's house. The whole family was together. I loved that. A* posada *is a nine-day celebration that begins on December 16 and ends on Christmas Eve. It's a religious celebration in which the nativity scene is displayed in the family's living room, usually around the Christmas tree. It represents the holy family: Joseph, Mary, Baby Jesus and the Holy Spirit that watches over them. We serve traditional foods like* tamales, posole, menudo *and* champurrado, *a hot beverage made out of seasonal fruits. We also have music and distribute bags of* bolos *(candy bags), and we break the* piñata. *The Christmas celebration doesn't end*

Michelle in Durango, 1990.

there. It's followed on January 6 by the celebration of the Three Wise Men and then on February 2 by the celebration of the Candelaria or the Epiphany.

We didn't stay very long in Mexico that time. I remember we moved back to the United States to live with my Aunt Ofelia in San Pedro. We stayed there for about a year and a half. There were nine people living in a two-bedroom house. My uncle and aunt lived in one bedroom, and the rest of us lived in the other one. My mom, sister and I slept in one bed, my Aunt Lupita and her daughter slept on a cot, and my cousins shared a bed. It was a crowded room. When my grandparents came from Mexico, they slept on a couch in the living room, and when my youngest uncle came, my grandparents shared the couch with him. I never questioned this. I thought it was normal. This is what we knew. I started kindergarten in San Pedro.

I loved it when the bus made stops at different cities along the routes. I loved watching the people.

When I was six years old, we moved back to Mexico to live with my grandparents. My mom never explained why we were moving, but at that time I thought that moving was pretty normal. Whenever we traveled back and forth from Mexico to the United States, we always took a bus. At first we took the Greyhound Bus, but later we took a bus named Tres Estrellas. Since we came as tourists, we could only bring two or three outfits and a pair of shoes in our brown suitcase. That was it. On the bus, we always wore comfortable clothes, like sweat pants,

Fiorela, eleven years old, in Los Angeles, 1997.

never jeans. The first leg of the trip was from Los Angeles to El Paso, Texas. In El Paso, we usually took a cab to cross the border to Ciudad Juarez and then would go to the Central Station to get a bus to Durango. The trip from Durango to Gomez Palacio took ten hours. I know this because we still make the trip. The bus had a bathroom, but you wouldn't want to go there. We used the bathroom at the bus station instead.

The full trip was long and boring, about twenty-four hours. We never brought any toys. I remember one time the only thing we had to play with was a pack of gum. The only other thing I could do was to look out the window, but there was nothing to look at but hills. My mom always bought two tickets instead of three to save money. My mom would sit on the aisle; my sister would sit in the middle. I would sit in the crack between them since I didn't have a seat. It was very uncomfortable. I couldn't stretch my legs. If I moved I would hit my sister or my mom. I was stiff the whole time, and whenever we got off the bus, every part of my body hurt. But as I got older, I looked forward to the trips. I loved it when the bus made stops at different cities along the routes. I loved watching the people.

I have a lot of good memories of Mexico. When we were living in the United States, we slept on the floor, but at my grandparents' home, we had beds. It felt like home. I knew that there would always be someone at home waiting for me, usually my grandmother who was cooking. I still remember those smells coming out of the kitchen. There was always a lot of family around. The concept of "latch-key kid" doesn't exist in Mexico like here. We often stayed up late at night with my older cousins, and sometimes my grandpa would come outside on the porch and play his guitar. I felt normal and safe with the whole family close to me. My sister and I had a lot of friends in the neighborhood. It was always safe to go outside, no matter what time. In Mexico, everyone becomes family, and if something happens, there is always someone to help.

When I was about seven years old, we moved back to San Pedro, stayed a short time and then moved to Los Angeles to live with my Aunt Ofelia. My mom, sister and I shared one room, and my grandparents stayed in a room in the back of the house whenever my grandfather came for work. It was hard living there because there were always arguments and conflicts, and people were always coming and going. Since we were living in their house, we had to hold back our feelings. We couldn't complain. We felt like we were intruders.

By this time, I was tired of not having my own house. I felt different from the other kids. I was aware of the fact that I was living in two different countries and felt that I didn't belong in either place. I wanted stability. When you're a child, you need stability and when you don't have it, you feel confused. I didn't want to think about things. The only one I could share my feelings with was Fiorela. I suffered a lot, but she suffered more. She blamed our hard times on our parent's separation. My sister was always more sensitive about my dad. Not having a father changed everything for her. I felt that I had to be the strong one, and I always tried to listen and comfort her.

Mexicans are fascinated by Americans. They think everyone is rich.

We saw my dad a few times during this time and then didn't see him again until I was fourteen and Fiorela was fifteen. He wanted me to treat him like a dad, but I couldn't because he was a stranger to me. At the end of the tenth grade, my sister and I went back to Mexico with our grandmother and found out that he had been married before my mom and had two daughters with that wife. It broke our hearts to find that out. When we got back to Los Angeles, we told our dad that we knew about his wife and daughters back in Mexico. He said, "Don't start." A week later he told us that he had another partner in the United States and that she had a son. We hadn't known any of this. Now he makes excuses not to see us. Now, if he talks to us, he does, and if he doesn't, too bad for him.

When I was eleven years old, my grandparents convinced my mom to move back to Mexico again because they were worried about her living alone with my sister and me. I was scared at first. I didn't know if the other kids would accept me. But word spread quickly that I was from Los Angeles, and everyone had a lot of questions for me. What's life like in L.A.? What do they eat? What do they do? Mexicans are fascinated by Americans. They think everyone is rich. Everyone wanted to be my friend. I was very popular, and all the girls told me that I had pretty clothes.

This time back in Mexico, I felt different from the other kids. I began to realize that I was part of two different cultures. I didn't know the Mexican holidays or customs. The Mexican pledge of allegiance was strange, and in school it was hard to speak and write only in Spanish. The schools in Mexico were also different. In Mexico, the schools are much poorer than here. Parents have to pay for everything—field trips, parties, construction paper and supplies. The walls in the classroom are plain with nothing to encourage the students to succeed. There are no assemblies. Nothing extra. Just a classroom with a board and seats. That's it. The teachers are also stricter. They expect their students to be responsible, respectful, and to act like young adults. The students know where the boundaries of respect are. When an adult enters the classroom, students have to stand.

In Mexico, I started going out with friends. I loved that. In Los Angeles, I never went to my friends' houses. My mom was gone most of the day working so she couldn't take us. I loved being in school, and I always got good grades. I was also more involved in activities outside of school, and my mother was more involved with school, which she couldn't do when I was younger. I also liked living with my grandparents. My favorite time was dinner time because the whole family would eat together and talk about their day. There was always laughter around the table, and my uncles would love to pick on me. I didn't feel lonely. We weren't suffering anymore. We felt we could live a normal life. I was happy.

But then after six months, my mother decided to return to Los Angeles again. She couldn't make it financially and she thought that we would have a better future in the United States. I was angry at my mom and sad that we had to leave. All I wanted was a normal life. I didn't want any more changes. My sister and I felt that Mexico was our home, and we knew it would be hard going back to sleeping on the floor. When we left Mexico, my sister and I cried. It broke our hearts. My sister and I were the only ones who understood each other. We were close because of all the moving around.

When we went back to the United States, we lived with my Aunt Ofelia in Rosemead. I didn't like Rosemead. I didn't like my school. I didn't feel like I fit in because none of my classmates had the same experiences as I had. Every day I prayed that we would go back to Mexico. There were a few Latinos in Rosemead, but they were second-generation immigrants. I was first-generation. I didn't like my teacher. I didn't participate in class because he made me feel dumb. He thought that since I had lived in Mexico, I couldn't speak English very well. I remember feeling anxious in class, waiting for the day to end. I was an outsider. I didn't have many friends. Also we didn't have too many clothes. My mother couldn't buy us clothes because there were other things she had to buy, like food. Clothes were the last thing on the list. My sister told me that she felt embarrassed because she had to wear the same thing more often than the other kids. I was luckier because I wore a uniform.

When I was thirteen, we moved back to our old neighborhood in Los Angeles,

I was always starting over. I was tired of moving back and forth and just wanted to settle down.

and I started middle school. I still had friends from when I was in elementary school, but I hadn't seen them in many years. I was the new girl watching from the sidelines. I was quiet most of the time. Moving around made me feel lost and made me lose confidence. I didn't know how to combine my two cultures, being Mexican but also being American. I was beginning to get used to Mexican customs when we lived in Mexico, but then we moved back and I had to start over. I was always starting over. I was tired of moving back and forth and just wanted to settle down. Even though it was hard going back and forth, I never let it affect my school grades. I always wanted to be at the top of my class. Some children might have given up but I didn't. As a child I felt helpless most of the time, and I knew that the only way I would get out of my situation was to get myself through school.

It was also difficult because I was becoming a teenager, and teenagers are different in Mexico than here. Here they grow up fast. They do things without thinking. In Mexico, kids are more relaxed and calm. They remain children longer. We had a lot of fights with my mom. I wanted to fit in and do what the other girls were doing, like going to school dances and hanging out. I wanted to spend more time outside of the home. My mom wasn't ready for that. She was very protective. We had a lot of differences. American children are accustomed to their independence. Their parents accept their personality and views. It's different in Mexican families. Parents accept their kids' personalities, but not the views. You are expected to accept the views and values of your parents.

The movie Spanglish *deals with some of these cross-cultural problems. There is a scene at the end of the movie when the mother, who is from Mexico, tries to talk with her daughter. As the mother walks toward her, the daughter puts up her hand and says, "Not now. I*

Michelle and María in Mexico, 2007.

need my space." To which the mother responds, "There is no space between mother and daughter." Mexican families do not believe in space. The movie also shows how it feels to translate for your parent. I always knew that I had to translate for my mom. I know she must have felt frustrated and embarrassed because her daughters had to speak for her. I could see it was a struggle for her. But I'm supposed to be the kid.

By the time I started high school, I considered myself to be an American, and I began to have my own values and morals. For a while I even questioned my religion, which naturally my mom didn't like. It was hard because my mother thought that if my sister or I did something wrong, it was her failure as a parent. She had different experiences growing up and couldn't relate to our lives. She would ask herself: Why can't I understand my child? My sister would tell my mother that she needed to learn from her mistakes, but my mom would say, "But I'm your mother." My mom has come to accept our lifestyle. She has become more open-minded. My sister and I encourage her to take risks, like learning how to drive or going back to school to learn a new career. This is a work in progress.

In June of 2006, I graduated from high school, and in the fall I enrolled at California State University at Northridge. My major is child development, but I've also been thinking about studying political science. My interest in political science developed in high school where I became active in political campaigns and volunteered at City Hall. I began to see the inequities that exist for minorities living in the United States. Many Latinos are under-represented in our political system, and I would like to see that change. Latinos are also the least likely to vote, although slowly we are beginning to step up.

Michelle's Reflections

I feel that I am part of two very different cultures. The American part is that I am very independent. I have my goals. I want to pursue them, and I am encouraged to pursue them. I am very determined. I am also proud of being Mexican. My heart and my soul are Mexican. But I don't think I could live in Mexico because my thinking is more American. Mexicans are raised to accept what they have and to be grateful for what they have, which is how my grandmother raised my mother and my mother raised my sister and me. Americans are different. They feel that they can accomplish anything in life. They are encouraged to pursue their dreams. And they always want more, more, more. I was talking with my cousin about my dreams and plans and when I asked about hers, she had no response. She doesn't aspire to any dream. I think that is sad.

But I have also noticed that children of immigrants sometimes put down their own culture. They think that American culture is the "right culture," and

Los Angeles. Top: Michelle, María, Fiorela, Bottom: Catarino, Hortencia, 2008.

acting American is the "right" way to act. They want to be accepted and liked, which is natural, but they get so carried away with material things and running their own successful lives that they don't look around and see how they can help their families and communities. They have become individualistic. They only care about themselves and only focus on their needs and wants. They don't see that there are people who don't have what we have. Mexican culture does not support the idea of individualism. We were raised to always put the needs of our family first. In Mexico the family is everything.

I would like to get married in the future, but I feel that it would be hard to find someone who can accept me. I am very independent, and most Latino boys are raised in the machismo way. In the past, machismo was not considered to be a bad thing. It meant being able to protect and support your family. Today machismo is viewed as being superior to women. A man with machismo is considered to be a sexist who wants to control his relationship. I do not want that. I'm looking for someone who respects me as a person and accepts and encourages me with my career. I want to have a relationship where we can both learn to trust each other and make decisions as a couple. I want someone I can share my life and dreams with. Maybe I'm asking for too much, but here in the United States, men and women are equal and have the same opportunities. Women can choose to stay at home or continue with their profession. I will definitely continue with my education, and then if marriage comes, it comes, but if it doesn't, I'm okay with that.

I have many dreams. I want to graduate from college and continue with my Master's and obtain a doctorate in education or political science. Either way I would like to work in education. I want to do positive things for my community and help people. I love the feeling of knowing you have helped people achieve and have a better life. When I see the struggles of low-income Latino families, it reminds me of what I went through with my mom. One of my dreams is to continue to travel and see new places. I would also love to help my cousin fulfill her dream to come here and go to school.

I am pretty sure that if I had stayed in Mexico, my dreams would have been limited. I probably would have struggled to attend college, and since college is expensive, I would have picked something like secretarial work. It might have been important to marry and have a family. I have gained so much by living here. My mom made the right choice in deciding to live here. She thought about her decision carefully. She wanted to go where my sister and I would have a better future, and she knew it would be easier and better for us in the United States. She is proud that I'm going to college but also a little nervous about my future. My grandfather is very proud that I am going to a university and working to become a professional. He has sacrificed a lot to give his family a better life. It frustrates me that Americans don't see how hard Mexican people work. He told me, "I grew up in the fields. That's all I knew. You grew up in Los Angeles, where you can live a better life than most people in Mexico."

Thuynga's Story

Thuynga Nguyen was born in Nam Dinh, North Vietnam, on October 20, 1952. In 1954, after the communist regime took power from the French, Thuynga's family fled to South Vietnam. After the Vietnam War ended, life did not improve. Living under the communist government was difficult, especially because her husband had worked for the prior regime. In 1987, Thuynga, her husband and two children in secret boarded a boat to Malaysia. Crammed under the deck with seventy-five other refugees, they feared not only the ocean storms but also Thai pirates noted for robbing and raping women. After spending twenty months in Malaysia, they came to the United States, where they live today. Here is Thuynga's story.

Thuynga

Historical Note:
French influence in Vietnam goes back to the 1700s when French missionaries began arriving in Vietnam, but the French occupation did not begin until 1858. At that time, following several military conquests, the entire country of Vietnam came under French control and was renamed Indochina. Resistance to the occupation quickly developed, the first of any note being the establishment of the Vietnam Quoc Dan Dang Party. This was followed in 1941 by the emergence of the Viet Minh, which was an umbrella group of parties led by a young revolutionary named Ho Chi Minh.

During World War II, Japan invaded Vietnam. The Japanese kept in place the Vichy French colonial administration as its puppet government. In 1945, following the defeat of the Japanese, the Viet Minh proclaimed a provisional government in Hanoi. In that same year, the French sent the French Far East Expeditionary Corp to Vietnam to restore its rule, leading to the First Indochina War between the Viet Minh and the French forces. On May 8, 1954, the French were defeated after the battle of Dien Bien Phu. The Geneva Conference of 1954 ended France's occupation of Vietnam and divided the country in half at the seventeenth parallel. The communists took control of the Democratic Republic of Vietnam (DRV) in the north, and the nationalists controlled the Republic of Vietnam in the south (RVN). The Geneva Accords also called for general elections in 1956 to unify the country, but fearing the possible victory of Ho Chi Minh, the United States and South Vietnam would not allow these elections to take place.

My Parents

My father, Lich, was born in 1904, and my mother, Sen, in 1908. My parents were from different villages outside of the city of Nam Dinh in North Vietnam. This was a rural area so probably their families had been farmers. Education was important in my father's family, and he finished high school, which was unusual at that time. Most children did not even finish elementary school. My father was a writer and poet although he never published anything;

During that time, women didn't have any expectations; they just followed their husbands. They really didn't have their own dreams.

he just wrote for fun. He was a very funny man, and his stories were passed on from family to family. Everyone loved listening to them because he could talk to any generation. He died in Vietnam when he was 101 years old. I was living in the United States.

My mother was fortunate to have a family who understood that if she could read and write, she would have more opportunities. At that time only men went to school. Typically when young girls reached seven or eight years of age, they were taking care of their younger brothers or sisters and helping to run the household so their parents could go out and make a living. My mom's family sent her to a tutor's house to study. She finished the third grade, just enough education to be able to work. During that time, women didn't have any expectations; they just followed their husbands. They really didn't have their own dreams.

My parents lived in a small community where everybody knew each other. Marriages were arranged at that time, and my grandfather had a friend who knew a family that had a son. They played matchmaker, and when my mother was sixteen and my father was twenty, they got married. My mother was very sweet and known in the community for her beauty.

My family was Catholic. My parents had thirteen children, including me, but three died before I was born so I only grew up with ten. My mother's first child was born when she was seventeen and the last child when she was forty-three. There are twenty-six years between the oldest and youngest child. When I was born, one sister already had a family. I have a nephew who is older than I am.

In 1954, when I was two years old, my family fled to the south. When my father was a young man, he was part of a revolutionary group that was fighting against the French. He was a patriot who loved his country and wanted Vietnam to be run by Vietnamese, but he didn't believe in communism. Around this time, the communist leader, Ho Chi Minh, was rising in power, and some people confused communism with patriotism. When the group my father belonged to became communist, he resigned. He felt he had no choice but to leave the north.

Millions of people were fleeing the north at this time. The government let people decide if they wanted to leave, but there was an unspoken pressure to stay. There were no ports where my family lived so we had to travel to Hai Phong. We couldn't go as a family. People would have been suspicious. So, two of my brothers, a sister and I went with my parents, and the four older brothers went with their school.

My father's brother was in a position to help my family escape. He was well off financially and could help with transportation. Because he had been recruited by the communists, he had knowledge about escape routes. He knew he should leave but he also knew that because he was a prominent man, they would be looking for him. At that time, anyone with property was rounded up and put into jail. Even though he had helped the communists, there was no loyalty. He was still a landowner. He ended up dying in jail. Everyone in my mother's family moved to the south, and everyone in my father's family stayed in the north. We had absolutely no contact with my father's family until 1975, not even letters.

My Life in South Vietnam

My family first moved to Dalat City, (north of Saigon, now known as Ho Chi Minh City), and then in 1959, when I was seven years old, we moved to a neighborhood in Saigon. At that time, Saigon was not a big city. There weren't a lot of people. There were no big buildings at all. There weren't even many bicycles. Everyone in my neighborhood got along. If you were Catholic, you went to church, and if you were Buddhist, you went to temple. We

> *Historical Note:*
> *Ho Chi Minh City (formerly Saigon) is the largest city in Vietnam. In 2007, there were six million people living there. It is also the commercial center of the country.*

coexisted. In Vietnam the main religions are Catholic and Buddhism, but Buddhist ideas of respecting and honoring your ancestors became a big part of Vietnamese culture, and even people who weren't Buddhist honored their ancestors through prayer.

My father opened a small store, like a convenience store. It started out as a bookstore but my father couldn't make enough business selling books, so he began to rent books instead, which wasn't very successful either. The store was in front of the first floor of our house. We had a living room, kitchen and a bathroom in the back of the house. On the second floor, there was one large bedroom full of beds. I shared a bed with my sister. The boys shared a bigger bed.

For the first few years, I didn't go to school because my father home-schooled me. He taught me how to read, write and do math, and he taught me French as well, which he had learned growing up in the north. All of my brothers and my sister went to Catholic school and Vu, one of my brothers, became a priest. He

*In Vietnam we say,
"Parents give us the body,
but teachers give us the mind
and the knowledge."*

left Vietnam in 1965 to study in France and never came back to live in Vietnam. In 1960, when I was eight, my parents sent two of my brothers and me to a Catholic boarding school in Vung Tau, which was about two hours from my house by car. I was there for three years and then came back home for high school.

Education was very important to my parents. We had many books at home and my whole family loved to read. My brother and my father made all of us read one book a month. Sometimes my dad would pick out the book, but we had so many that sometimes we would pick our own. He would even make us write a report when we finished the book. Everybody in my family had to go to college. They told us that if we had a good education, we would have a good job and a good life. In Vietnam we say, "Parents give us the body, but teachers give us the mind and the knowledge." We teach our children that if they want a good life they need to study, not to make money but to have knowledge so they can be good people.

1963: The Assassination of President Diem

The assassination of President Diem took place on All Saints Day so everyone was off. Typically on a holiday, my entire family would come to the house and have a huge meal. We were getting ready for lunch and all of a sudden we heard gun shots. We looked out the window and saw police cars everywhere. My house was across the street from the police headquarters. We were very scared. We didn't know what to expect. The radio announced that there was a rebellion

Historical Note:
President Ngo Dinh Diem, who was Catholic and Confucian, became president of the Republic of Vietnam in 1955. Some felt that Diem discriminated in favor of Catholics, which brought about protest from religious advocates. One Buddhist priest burned himself to death in protest. President Kennedy, concerned that Diem could hurt anti-communist efforts, did not intervene when in 1963 a group of generals overthrew President Diem and assassinated him and his brother. Following this, the country entered into a period of political instability with one government quickly replacing another. Three weeks after the assassination of President Diem, President Kennedy was also assassinated. Lyndon B. Johnson, Kennedy's Vice President, immediately took over, pledging to continue the policies of the Kennedy Administration. In 1967, Nguyen Van Thieu was elected President of South Vietnam, ending the military coups that began after the assassination of President Diem.

against the president. It wasn't until the next day that we found out that they had killed the president and his advisor, who was his brother. The military took over. My parents talked to us about this, but I was very young, so I wasn't really interested. What I do remember is that school was cancelled, so we got to stay home.

People felt that the Americans were behind the assassination. President Diem was assassinated in 1963, and in 1964 a flood of Americans started coming, so it was natural for people to believe that the Americans were involved. There was talk about a "domino effect." The Americans were worried that they needed to hold on to Vietnam, or communism would spread to Laos, Cambodia, and other Southeast Asian countries. I don't think President Diem agreed with this. He was very nationalistic and against the Americans coming to Vietnam. He wanted to keep Vietnam free from foreigners. He was well respected because he was viewed as a person who really loved Vietnam.

1964-1965: Americans Started Coming

Little by little, the Americans continued to come, and then in 1965 there were many Americans in Saigon. My earliest memory of the war is that all of a sudden the city was transformed to accommodate the American soldiers. There was a lot of bustle. There was a lot of construction, lots of tall buildings being built. They were also building roads, bridges and housing for the soldiers. There was also a lot of journalists in the city. I remember all the bars that started opening up. Bars became part of the social atmosphere. Before that there had been no bars. There had been venues where there were singers, but not any bars until the Americans came. The bad thing was that because of the bars, there was also prostitution. Prior to that, I hadn't seen any prostitution. Most of these women came from the countryside to work in Saigon and send money to their families. They could never tell their families or people in their neighborhoods what they did. There was definitely a cultural stigma, but the women felt they had to do what they had

Historical Note:
The United States became involved in Vietnam as early as 1950 to assist the French colonial forces, and from 1954 to 1973 deployed military personnel and economic assistance to South Vietnam. In 1965, President Johnson sent large numbers of combat troops. By 1969, there were more than 553,000 American soldiers. That same year President Johnson also began bombing North Vietnam.

Australia, New Zealand, South Korea, Thailand, the Philippines and Taiwan also sent troops. China and the Soviet Union backed the North Vietnamese with weapons and other aid.

to do. Prostitution was not the first choice for women, but for some women this was the only way they could make a living and feed their families.

I felt that the Americans were there to help and do good things for our country, but there were people who felt that the Americans were just as controlling as the communists. On the one hand, people were trying to flee from the communists in the north, and on the other hand, there was a strong American hold in the south. In high school, students never brought up the war. It was not part of the curriculum so it was not spoken about. We were aware that there were American protests against the war, and in Vietnam at many colleges there were demonstrations and debates over the war. I didn't participate because politics was a male arena. I didn't like the war. Nobody was in support of the war. Most wars are about one country fighting another, but this war was about one family fighting another, one part of a country fighting the other part. It was my brothers and sisters who were dying.

Other than having the Americans in the city, life was normal. For the most part, because we were in Saigon, we didn't see any combat. Everyone was civil. My brother Rao was a journalist, and he often brought journalists and people he was interviewing to our home. The economy was better because of the influx of Americans. People rented out parts of their homes to Americans, and people were able to sell things to them that the Vietnamese wouldn't pay for. Another change was that many people living in the villages moved into the city for jobs. They were able to make a living and send money back home to their families. Also, a lot of American businesses came to Vietnam. People who had education could double their salary if they worked for the Americans. Before my husband was drafted, he worked as an interpreter for the officers of the 7th Division of the United States Air Force in Pleiku, in central Vietnam.

1968: The Tet Offensive

There was no fighting in Saigon until the Tet Offensive in 1968. Tet is the New Year so the day started off really happy. For the New Year's holiday, everybody is off work for three days. Everyone comes home to have a meal with the family. All the streets on that day were empty because the stores and schools

Historical Note:
In 1968, North Vietnam attacked suddenly and secretly over the Vietnam New Year in hopes of sparking an uprising among the South Vietnamese. All South Vietnam's major cities received heavy damage. The Tet Offensive was a turning point in the war. Many Americans began to see the war as impossible to win and urged leaders to end United States' involvement. The Tet Offensive also effectively ended the political career of President Johnson, who chose not to run for re-election. On May 10, 1968, the first peace talks began in Paris between the United States and the Democratic Republic of Vietnam.

were closed. The fighting started in the afternoon and was scattered throughout Saigon. People stayed in their homes. We heard gunshots or bombs in the distance. It trickled into Saigon. We were afraid to go out on the street because there could be a bomb. Because it was New Year, we had stocked our homes with food, so we didn't have to leave the house. My family stayed inside for about one week. Everything in the city was closed—the school, the stores, everything. I was really scared. I heard rockets go off day and night. To get our news, we listened to the radio and watched television.

After the Tet Offensive, the government needed more men to join the military. Two of my brothers, Cau and Rao, were called up. Cau, who had been a French teacher, went to work in the military academy where they trained soldiers. After the war, he went to prison for three years. My brother Rao, who was almost thirty-five years old, had written for *United Press International (UPI)*, the *New York Times* and the *Washington Post*. After his initial training, he began writing for the military, but he didn't feel that he could be honest, and because he was drafted, he couldn't leave.

In 1970, Rao knew he had to escape. He decided to go to France because by this time two of our brothers, Vu and Hoa, were living there. When Rao arrived at the airport, his brothers grabbed him. They were afraid that someone would take him away. It took four or five days for Rao to call home. My parents were so scared. My father didn't tell me anything until my brother was safe. Rao originally had wanted to come to America, but there were immigration laws dictating that if you came to America without proper documentation, the government would

Family photo taken in Saigon when Thuynga was twenty, 1972. Thuynga is in the top row, third from the left. Her father is second from the right in the top row. Thuynga's mother is in the bottom row, second from the left.

send you back to your own country, and France didn't have that law. His safe haven was in France.

I didn't realize how dangerous it was. My brother left his gun in our house and told my father that once he reached France, my father should take it apart and throw the pieces in the sewer. My brother was afraid that the military would find the gun, and he didn't want my family to get involved. My friend read that the military was looking for my brother because they thought he was a Viet Cong.

Getting Married

There are really only two paths for most Vietnamese girls. You either go to the convent or you get married. By twenty, you need to be married. After twenty-three or twenty-four if you aren't married, people think there is something wrong with you. People will start to talk. They will think that you are not a good person or you have issues. There is a stigma. After your thirties it's hard for you to get married. That's the culture.

There are really only two paths for Vietnamese girls. You either go to the convent or you get married.

At the time I graduated, women basically got their degree in order to marry someone else with a degree and live their lives through their husbands. Even if you had a college degree, or a post-degree, even if you were a doctor, you pretty much ended up having a family, and whatever aspirations you had were put on the back burner. There's a joke that women get their college degrees to hang them in the kitchens of their houses. That was the life women had.

I met my husband Tho at my sister's wedding. He was a friend of my brother-in-law. I was looking for a husband at that time, and he seemed like a good fit. At the beginning, he would come to my house to talk, and then after one or two months, we went out together, usually for lunch or a movie. We took things slowly. Vietnamese courting is still that way. Eight months after meeting, we got married.

The morning of my wedding, my husband's family brought wine, cakes and jewelry to my family's home, which is our custom. That tradition is carried on today. I had a traditional wedding, pretty big for that time. On my wedding night my husband and I moved in with his family. There's no independent living in Vietnam. You can't just go out and get an apartment like in America. You're bound to your parents. In Vietnam, the whole family lives in one household from grandparents to siblings. I wanted to live in my own house, not with my husband's family, but since my husband was the oldest son living at home, he felt he needed to stay so he could be close to his parents. In our culture, we respect and take care of old people.

My husband worked as an officer at the naval base and came home every other day. He had been studying to be a business lawyer and only had one more year left in college, but after the government changed the age to serve, he had to leave school. I was not fearful for him because he was on a large base close to the city and didn't see a lot of combat.

I kept myself busy. Every morning I went to church. After church, I cleaned the house and made tea for my father-in-law. Then I cleaned the yard and went shopping for the day's meals. Back then we went shopping every day to a wet market, not like here where you go to a grocery store once a week. Everything we ate was fresh. We had a refrigerator but only for drinks. I would bring home the food and leave it for two younger sister-in-laws who would later cook the meal for the family. After church and shopping, I went to work. I had

Thuynga's wedding in Saigon, 1974. She is twenty-two and her husband Tho is twenty-nine.

gone to college for two years, but quit because I didn't have time to both work and go to school. I found a job at the Ministry of Transportation as a computer programmer. When I started working for the deparment, there was only one supervisor and me, but over the years the department grew and grew, and I became an asset because they needed people in my field. I was grateful to have a job and kept it for many years. While I was living with my husband's family, my daughter Uyen was born.

On January 15, 1973, President Nixon announced the suspension of all offensive actions against the North Vietnamese and the withdrawal of the remaining United States forces. On January 27, the Paris Peace Accords were signed, ending direct United States involvement in Vietnam. Then in December 1974, the Congress passed the Foreign Assistance Act, which cut off all military aid to the South Vietnamese government. President Nixon resigned after the Watergate scandal, and his successor, Gerald Ford, was even less willing to continue supporting the war.

The last American troops left after the fall of Saigon in April of 1975. Though South Vietnam soldiers continued to fight, their defense was weakened when most American troops withdrew. The North set up a massive attack in early 1975 and continued to push toward Saigon. When their forces were about to topple the city, South Vietnam President Nguyen Van Thieu resigned. Duong Van Minh, one of the generals who had been involved in the assassination of President Diem, took over leadership. Though South Vietnamese troops stood ready to defend Saigon, Minh ordered surrender on April 25, 1975, saving the city from complete destruction. The Vietnam War finally ended on April 30 when Saigon, the capital of South Vietnam, fell to North Vietnamese forces.

There is debate over the number of people killed during the Vietnam War. Most agree that there were over 58,000 American soldiers killed, and another 45,000 wounded. The estimates of Vietnamese civilians killed range from two to almost six million, the majority from North Vietnam.

April 30, 1975: The Fall of Saigon

The night of April 30, I remember hearing rockets and gunfire going off. There was shooting at the airport. The next day there was chaos on the street. It seemed like the world had collapsed. I had no idea what was going to happen. I didn't know if my life would go on. I had just given birth to my daughter Uyen, who was only a month and a half old. I was afraid. I didn't see any future. Every man, woman and child tried to get out. People were running to the harbor looking for a ship to board. There were ships lined up and it was first come first served. The pictures on the news from Iraq remind me of Vietnam—the broken buildings, people lying on the streets, people crying. There were no phones so I couldn't contact anyone. I didn't know what had happened to my parents. I never thought that this would happen. I never thought that Saigon would fall. After a few months, I was able to contact my relatives in the north.

Two days before the fall of Saigon, my husband was sent home from the naval base. Some of his friends had already escaped, and others in his unit were sent to fight. We decided he should leave with his two younger brothers. We didn't think I was in danger if I stayed because we thought it would be safe for women and children. My husband and his brothers went to the harbor to look for a ship to board, but when he thought about me and his family, he decided he couldn't leave and came back home with his two brothers. My father-in-law was able to escape. Prior to coming to South Vietnam, he had been part of an anti-communist organization in North Vietnam. He was scared that if the new government caught him, they would find out that he had been a part of this organization and kill him. My sister Huong also escaped.

The chaos lasted for about one month. Everything was closed. There was no order anywhere. There was trash everywhere. People who were supposed to clean it were gone. Even if they reported to work, who was going to pay them? The streets were a mess. People did whatever they wanted. People set up shop wherever they wanted. There was no authority. Luckily we had enough food. In most houses there is usually a huge sack of rice and fish sauce. Slowly things got back to normal. At the time, I was so preoccupied with my baby that I didn't look too far into the future.

My Husband Goes to a Re-education Camp

After the Fall of Saigon, we didn't know what to expect. We knew we had lost the war, so we were waiting to see what would happen. After three months, the government put my husband in a re-education camp. The new government said that anyone who was a part of the old regime's military would have to report to them and would be sent away for ten days. For my husband, ten days turned into five years and one month. Many people died in the camps.

I didn't know where they took him. It was a long time before I got a letter from my husband, maybe three or four months later. There was no return address so I didn't know where it came from. It was a generic letter. It didn't say anything personal. He was unable to write about what was going on. Sometimes the government sent a letter telling us we could send a care package to the prisoners. They gave us a ticket.

Historical Note:
In 1976, now completely under Communist rule, Vietnam was officially reunited and named the Socialist Republic of Vietnam. Those who had held positions in the South Vietnamese government and others who were influential in religious or literary groups were sent to what was called "re-education camps," which were basically hard labor prison camps. Security and censorship were strict with bans on pre-1975 works in the fields of music, art and literature. Churches were all put under the control of the state, and anyone who spoke out was punished severely.

We would prepare what we wanted to send and bring it to the post office. We didn't know where it was going. We just had that ticket and somehow the package made its way to the camp. In camp, they only fed the prisoners rice, so I would send anything that had a long shelf life like dried shrimp, dried shredded pork, and sugar. Also, pork fat was a high commodity.

After about a year, my family was finally allowed to visit my husband. I went with my daughter, his older sister and younger sister. Even though we were from the city and had good clothes, we had to change into country clothing that was more suitable for visiting. We had to wear black pants and a normal shirt, nothing fancy. We took with us whatever we could carry, the more the better, because we didn't know when we would see him again. The first time I saw him he was really thin and very dark because he had been working in the field clearing out jungle so the government would have more land. It was sad to see that the government would use his labor and not give him anything in exchange. They wouldn't even feed him properly.

There was a feeling of camaraderie and shared experience that helped us get through this time.

The way I got through this was to have hope. You had to hope that your loved ones would be able to learn whatever they needed to learn so the government would release them. You lived day to day for that day.

Usually I would see the same people making that journey to the camps. There was a feeling of camaraderie and shared experience that helped us get through this time.We all became friendly, and through these connections, we would try and get more information about our loved ones. Many people didn't know what camps their loved ones were in, so when we would talk with our husbands, we were able to get news back to people on the other side. We didn't have permission to visit every month. Sometimes we would see him every month for four or five months and then nothing. Sometimes they would move him. Then we would receive a letter telling us where he was.

Life in Saigon after the War

In the beginning, the family was okay. I was still working at my old job. I was fortunate. All my friends who had husbands in the army or who worked for the previous government were fired. There was a law that if you were a wife of a former soldier, you were not allowed to work. But the vice president of the department, who had been a computer analyst in Russia, wanted to keep all of us in the computer group together. We could not live off the salary, but it was better than nothing at all. Work allowed me to stay in the city of Saigon. If you didn't work, you had to leave the city.

When the war ended, people who sensed there was trouble took their money out of the bank. After a while, the government changed the money so our money was worthless. We had nothing. In five years I had no new clothes. Things became harder with my husband's family. In the beginning, we had a good life so everybody felt at ease, but after 1975, there were so many difficulties. Earning a living was difficult. Everybody felt so much stress. It was really hard.

You used whatever you had. You never bought frivolous things; you used your money for food and necessities.

Sometimes we had to sell things for money. Every time my friend went to see her husband in the re-education camp, she had to sell her rings, jewelry and clothing to buy food for him and to pay for transportation. Everyone was very frugal, not knowing what was going to happen. You used whatever you had. You never bought frivolous things; you used your money for food and necessities. You lived day to day. I had to just wait for my husband to come back. What else was there for me to do?

In the summer of 1980, my husband got out of the camp. They released him early in the morning. By the time he got home, it was afternoon and I was still working. When I got home, I didn't know he was there because he was in the back of the house; then someone told me, "He's home. He's home."

1982: My Daughter and I Go to Prison

Within a few days after my husband was released, people were coming to us asking him to help people escape. They thought that because my husband had been a naval officer, he would know which water routes to use. The cost of escape was three or four bricks of gold, but because my husband could help, our family was allowed to go for free. We tried to escape as a family seven times, and my husband tried on his own four or five more times. We were caught three times. Two times they took my daughter and me to prison, but we got out the next day because I had a child with me. The last time, they put my daughter and me in prison for four months. My daughter was five years old. My husband had tried to escape with us, but when we were captured, he was able to get away because he was in a different group. My daughter and I were in the first group to go, and he was in the last group.

I was processed for prison at about 6 p.m. The jail closed each day at 4, and they had already handed out the last meal. They didn't give me or my daughter any food. Once I was in the holding cell, the women prisoners gave us their leftover food. They put all the women and children in one big room. If the child was a daughter, she would always stay with the mother. A son older than eight would go with his dad. If there was no father, the boy would have to live by himself in the jail.

The cell was four walls of cement. It held up to seventy people, but if more were caught, they would all be put in the cell. We were just packed in there. We had to rearrange ourselves so that everyone would fit on the floor. Sometimes there would be a foot next to your head. Everybody put a bit of cloth on the cement to make it more comfortable. There was a small hole for a restroom in one corner of the cell. It wasn't covered; it was just raised so that water could flow down like a drain. It was very dirty. Normally we would only use that at night. The last people who arrived at the prison would have to sleep near the drainage hole. During the day we would use the restrooms outside. We took showers together. There was no privacy. There were a lot of fleas. Usually when new people came in they were the main targets of the fleas. The joke was "the fleas are tired of us; they are getting some fresh blood."

Almost all of the women were in jail because they were trying to escape. I became close to one woman who had the same name as my daughter, Uyen. She was young and really cute. She was sentenced to eight years in prison for organizing people to escape. I was close to her because she was younger and hadn't been married, but she really loved my daughter and took care of her. There was another woman who was there for the same reasons. She was a little older and had a husband. She and the other women were the "heads" of the prison because they had been there the longest. They took care of things. They organized things.

In the morning, we had fifteen minutes of exercise. Then we would clean up and go to fetch water from a nearby well. Fetching water from the well was a big thing. For one thing, it gave you a chance to leave the cell. Also the men's prison was on the way to the well and there was hope that maybe your husband or family members might see you. There was no way otherwise to know whether your husband or wife was still in the same prison because they didn't notify you. You just hoped that someone saw you and would communicate that to other prisoners. After we brought the water back, we would shower and clean up. We also used the water to clean the prison. We had to sleep there. We had to keep things tidy. We did what we could to get through

In the beginning, my family couldn't visit us, but after about two weeks they allowed them to send care packages. When they finally let the family visit, there was a gate between us so we couldn't hug each other. The only way we could touch was to put our hands through the gates. My husband never came to visit because it was too dangerous. Three months after I arrived, when I was taking a shower, some older women told me they thought I was pregnant. I had some discomfort, but I thought that was because I was sleeping in a cramped space on a concrete floor. I missed a period but figured that it was because I was worried and stressed. I was probably about four months pregnant when I was released, but I wasn't released because I was pregnant. The rule was that all women without children and who were between the ages of sixteen and fifty-five had to work in the fields for at least two years before being released. Since I had a child and because they needed space for new inmates, they released me. My son, An, was born in 1983.

Other than death, we couldn't get any lower. We had to take the chance.

When I got out of prison, I knew we had to leave Vietnam. We were at rock bottom. I knew that if we tried to escape, there was a chance we would die, but it didn't matter. I had heard stories of women who had been raped by Thai pirates, but that didn't matter either. Other than death, we couldn't get any lower. We had to take the chance. We felt there was no future for our children. We lost the war; they won the war. There was no way our children could go to college or start their own life. There was really no choice. We had to leave.

For the next five years, my husband and I continued working, waiting for the right time to escape. My husband took whatever jobs he could find because each time we tried to escape he couldn't go back to what he was doing before. One time he was a woodworker, another a goldsmith. I stayed in my old job until the last time I tried to escape and was sent to prison. I think they knew all along that I was trying to escape, but they always let me stay anyway. But after the last time, they fired me after one week because I didn't come back to work. When I was released from prison, I went to work in a sewing factory.

In 1987, one of my husband's friends came to us with another plan to escape. At first my husband wasn't in favor of leaving. He was tired. He had already tried to escape many times, and each time he suffered many hardships. He was working as a goldsmith at the time and was making a decent living. Also, he had heard news about an immigration program for people who had been in the re-education program. He felt that he would definitely qualify and thought it would be safer for the family if they waited.

I talked him into going. The plan was different from the others. The organizers rented a bus from the Viet Cong, so if the government flagged down the bus, the driver would explain that it was a tourist bus. I knew that the government would ask the driver for paperwork, not the passengers. And I thought that if we went to the location and there was no ship, we could just turn around and go home. It seemed like a safer plan than the others.

By this time, I only had one sister, two brothers and my parents left in Vietnam. My sister Huong was living in Tennessee. She left for America the day Saigon fell. My brother Vu, who had become a priest, left for France in 1965, Hoa went in 1969, Rao escaped in 1970, and my younger brother Duy left in 1974. In 1980, Rao started paperwork for my parents to go to France but my mother passed away in 1981. My father ended up going to France in 1983 and lived there for ten years before coming back to Vietnam.

My Family Escapes from Vietnam

On December 20, 1987, we left our home very early in the morning. The sky was still dark. We walked a block and a bus picked us up on the corner. The bus went to different locations where it picked up five or six people at each stop, a total of about fifty. Each person had one small bag. My husband and I brought one change of clothes and a few changes of clothes and food for my children. My son was four and my daughter twelve at that time. My son didn't know what was going on, but because my daughter had been in prison with me, she knew something was going on. It was exciting for her. She saw it as an adventure.

We arrived at Can Tho City at 4 p.m. and then rode around the city for about three hours until it was dark. The organizers separated us by groups. My group included my family and two other people who came on at the same bus stop. We were dropped off at a site where a person was waiting to take us to someone's home. When we got there, the owner said that six people were too many, and sent two people to a different house. We stayed at the house until we received instructions to move to another house, where there were about ten people. With each move, we were making our way to the shore to board the ship. Once at the shore, about thirty people boarded a small motorboat that took us to the large ship. Seventy-five people, including twenty children, were on the ship. Four people steered the boat, including my husband. They were our crew.

Historical Note:
Over one million people secretly escaped Vietnam during the period after the war. Those who went by boat were called Boat People. Many died at sea due to poor quality boats, sea pirates who raped and murdered, bad weather, hunger and thirst. Often refuges were stockpiled in camps in Thailand, Malaysia, Hong Kong, the Philippines and Indonesia for years. Eventually, most of them found asylum in the United States, Canada, Australia, France, West Germany, and Britain. In the 1990s, those who could not find a country that would accept them were deported back to Vietnam.

When we finally boarded, it was dark. I remember that it was a little eerie, pretty scary. There were smaller boats on the sea, mostly merchant ships. We had to hide under the deck to make sure that no one suspected that there were a lot of people on our ship because the word might get out. My family was fortunate because we had gotten on the ship early when there was still a lot of room. As more people got on, it became cramped. My daughter sat next to me, and when she was tired, she would lean on me. My son sat on my lap. Most children sat on their mother's lap; they didn't get their own space. I remember that I couldn't move my leg. If I needed to move, I had to ask the people next to me. We were all in this together so we knew we had to help each other to survive. It hurt so much.

If you were in the middle, there was no place to lean. We had to be completely quiet. The

We had to be completely quiet. The children could not make any sounds. Sometimes we couldn't even breathe.

children could not make any sounds. Sometimes we couldn't even breathe. Some people gave medicine to the children to help them sleep, but my children were so tired they didn't need medicine. We had some rice and water and dry fish, but no one wanted to eat. There were so many people that it became suffocating. When the people steering the ship thought it was safe, they would crack the deck a little to get some fresh air, but it was just a little crack of air. When it was dangerous, they would shut it again. I remember the feeling of being suffocated.

When we set sail, I noticed that the water on the shore was light green. People said that once we were out to sea, the water would turn blue, so when we saw blue water, everyone was happy and thought we were on our way out of Vietnamese waters. Then after a while we saw the water turning a little green again, and nobody knew what was going on. My husband was using the ship's navigation system to steer the ship, but it turned out that it was broken, which meant that all this time we were drifting back to the shore. Everyone was terrified. At that point, my husband had to navigate by the stars to get back to the ocean. He knew how to do this because he had been a naval officer in Vietnam.

Once we hit the ocean, there was a huge storm. There was a lot of motion. The ship was rocking back and forth. A huge wave hit the ship. Water was coming in everywhere. Everyone got wet. Nobody ate; nobody went to the restroom; nobody moved. My kids were really tired so they fell asleep. Then a second wave hit. Everybody grabbed buckets to get the water out of the ship. People were yelling and screaming. I was so scared that I passed out until the next morning.

When I woke up the next morning, the sea was still and it was sunny again. We were out of Vietnamese waters. We opened the deck so people could get some fresh air and use the bathroom. Everybody woke up slowly, so there wasn't one moment when we realized that we were out of Vietnamese waters. There was a slow ripple effect as everyone realized this. Some of the younger women changed their clothes and dolled up a little. It felt like there was new life on the ship. We all felt hope.

That evening, there was another scary moment. There was a smaller ship that seemed to be following us. It was going very fast. We didn't know what it was, but we thought that it could be a pirate ship. Suddenly everyone ran downstairs as fast as they could. All the women on the ship were terrified because they had heard stories about Thai pirates who would rob, kill and rape women who were escaping. We heard stories about women who ripped holes in their clothing and put dirt all over themselves so the pirates wouldn't want them. Slowly we saw the distance between us and the boat getting wider and wider, and then we felt a little more at ease. But at that moment people were preparing for the worst.

The morning of December 24, we saw another boat. Everybody immediately thought, "Oh no, this is it. This is the end for us." Again we thought they were pirates. All the women went under deck. We all prayed. Whatever religion you were, you prayed, and you hoped that this wasn't the end, that there was still something left for us. But seeing that boat chase after us, we were pretty frightened. The boat came right next to our ship. We could see that they were dark people. We didn't know who they were. It turned out that it was a Malaysian fishing vessel. The person manning the ship spoke English. He asked if we needed water. We still had water and were suspicious of their motives so we said we didn't need any, but when they offered us some fish, we realized that they were honest and good-natured and wanted to help. They told my husband that we were in Malaysian waters, about five or six hours from shore. They confirmed that the route my husband was taking was the right one.

We Arrive in Malaysia

Around 6 in the evening, we started to see the outline of the mountains in Malaysia. Everybody was really happy. We could see the lights on the houses and little mopeds that were driving along the coast. We followed the land, continuing toward shore until we crashed onto the beach. The engine stopped and some of the men jumped off to see how high the water level was. The water came up to their calves. Then there was a scurry of people wanting to jump. My husband was scared that the ship might flip over if everyone jumped out of the boat, so he stopped people from mass jumping and tried to get some order. He wanted all the women with children to get out first. Slowly everyone came out. The water was cold, but we didn't feel anything. When we got on the beach, I said to everybody I saw, "Merry Christmas, Merry Christmas," but they didn't say anything. Do you know why? They were Muslims.

The police gathered us together on the beach. They took a head count and roped us off. We were there for an hour and then took a bus to a location like a military base. We slept outside on a cement floor with tents. They handed everyone pieces of thin plastic. We used two to lie on and two for blankets. It was very cold that night. My husband was off with the other men, figuring out our plan.

When morning came, the authorities gave each of us a small carton of water, a bag of crackers and either dried raisins or dates. Then we went to a transfer camp for three or four days to wait for the ship to take us to the island of Pulo Bidong. The ship was called the "chicken ship" because it was a cargo ship that carried chickens. Once on the island, we were assigned to a housing complex and waited for the American delegation to complete our paperwork.

We stayed there for seven months. My husband worked in the United Nations

Commission's Piracy Unit, and every day I went to school to learn English, took care of the children, cooked and washed. My children went to school and learned English. Everybody knew each other, and there were friends from home. In the little laundry area, women would meet and become friends. We lived in what they called the "long house" with a lot of rooms. Two or three families shared a room; each had their own corner. Bathrooms were public. We cooked outside of the house. Life in that camp was basically about waiting to leave.

Classes on Life in America

While we were in the camp, they started to prepare us for life in America. The language and culture classes in Malaysia were a little off, but I didn't realize that until after I had lived in America. The main teacher was Vietnamese, but because they had so many students, they hired Malaysian people to also teach. My teacher was Malaysian. One lesson was about life in Chicago. The teacher kept on saying something about Chicago being "bumper-to-bumper." He couldn't explain what it meant, so I just went with it.

There was another lesson about bridal showers. When I first saw the words *bridal shower,* I thought it was about a bathing ritual. The bride had to get bathed. The teacher explained that at a bridal shower guests would throw confetti at the

This picture was taken in Malaysia the night the family left for the United States, September 1989. Thuynga's daughter and son are in front. Thuynga is second from the right in the first row, and her husband is next to her.

129

bride and groom while they were walking down the aisle. Looking back, I can laugh about our time in Malaysia, but at the time it seemed so overwhelming.

Although the Malaysian people were very kind and took us in, life in the camp was only a little less stifling than prison. I longed to be in America and have a life like my sister's. My sister sent pictures of her life in America. She always looked happy, and she wore nice clothes. There was freedom in America, and you could make an honest living. It seemed like a better life.

We left Malaysia on August 19, 1989, twenty months after we had escaped from Vietnam. Before we left, we had a little party to celebrate. We only had a little soda and cookies that we had around, but it was a big celebration. That night we took a short flight to Singapore, slept at the airport, and then flew from Singapore to Japan the next day. Slowly people parted ways. There were two families that flew to Hawaii. We flew to Seattle and then to Los Angeles. We had all been together and knew each other, but everybody was so happy that they were starting their own lives. None of us was sad.

My Family Arrives in America

We arrived in Los Angeles at night. My relatives came to pick us up at the airport, and as we were driving to their home, I saw all these houses and cars, things we used to see in movies. It was overwhelming. For the first week, we lived with my husband's family. The Catholic Church in Burbank had sponsored

This was a happy time for my family. We had freedom. For you, freedom doesn't mean much. But for us, it means everything.

my father-in-law and fifteen other families when they came here in 1975, the day Saigon fell. My husband's sisters and brothers joined him in the United States five years later in 1980. It was tough living with my husband's family because although there were three bedrooms, there were a lot of people living there. I felt like a stranger in that home. After one week, we moved into our own apartment.

This was a happy time for my family. We had freedom. For you, freedom doesn't mean much. But for us, it means everything. It didn't matter that we lived in a small apartment or that we had an old car. We had just come from a refugee camp, from nothing, zero. Here we were full of hope. At the beginning, I took things step by step so I wouldn't overwhelm myself. My life was about learning what I needed to survive. After we had been here for three months, my husband and I started adult school to learn English. Within a short time, I learned how to take the bus, how to order food from a fast-food restaurant, and how to use an ATM machine. After a year, I finally figured out how to pump my own gas. My sister-in-law took me to the grocery store and showed me where different foods were located. I remember thinking that the grocery stores here were really big. In Vietnam, the stores were much smaller. We joined the local Catholic Church. It was interesting. Mass was given in three languages: Spanish, English and Vietnamese. I taught Vietnamese to the children at the church.

The first Vietnamese friend I met here was the janitor of the Jewish Temple where I learned English. He was very helpful. He knew that my family had just arrived here and we didn't have anything so he gave us whatever he could: old tables, chairs, pots and pans, stuff that the church was getting rid of. He knew that I didn't know how to drive, so whenever he drove his wife to the market, he would ask me if I needed to go as well. This was very helpful to me. It was hard to go all the way to Chinatown without a car. We are still friends.

Historical Note:
There are approximately 1,643,000 Vietnamese living in the United States. The largest concentrations live in California (Orange County and the city of San Jose), and in Houston, Texas.

After ten months, we moved to Eagle Rock in the eastern part of Los Angeles. We reconnected with the brother of my husband's friend from Vietnam who offered to rent a house to us down the street from where he lived. It was a little more money then we were paying, but I told my husband we had to do this because we needed more space for the family. We didn't have the money but I said, "Let's just do it."

We had lots of Vietnamese friends who were living in Orange County at the time, and there definitely was a pull to move there, but I thought that if we were going to live in America we needed to live in a diverse area like Eagle Rock, so we could learn the language and culture. After a while, I noticed that Orange County had turned into a party tour where people would have parties all the time. This week one family would have a party and the next week another. It's good to have that, but I wanted some distance. I know people today who can barely speak English because in Orange County everyone speaks Vietnamese. You can go through your whole life and just speak Vietnamese.

My children had an easy time adjusting to life in America. They are more American than Vietnamese. They are fluent in English. They eat American food, like pizza and hamburgers, and they have friends from all over the world: America, the Philippines, China, Mexico and Vietnam. I think that's great. I want my children to feel comfortable with all cultures. That is part of the beauty of America.

At the same time, I didn't want them to forget their language and culture. That was important to me. I live in America, but I am Vietnamese. Yes, they may be American, but we don't look like the typical Americans. Our eyes and noses are different. If they go back to Vietnam, I want them to be comfortable in their homeland and be able to speak their language and blend in with their people. That is why we speak Vietnamese at home and celebrate Vietnamese holidays. I want my children to know about all the customs and foods that go along with the holidays. For example, on New Year we eat candied fruits, and for Middle Autumn we eat moon cakes.

Working in America

For the first year, I worked at home. My husband helped me. When we got here we were on the welfare program, but the money from the government was not enough, so we had to work. I made pants but specialized in making tricky pockets that not a lot of people have the skills to do. In Vietnam, everyone learns how to sew. I helped support the family as a seamstress for four years while my husband went to school to study computers. When he finished college, he applied for many jobs but couldn't find any in the field. He was so disappointed, but he had to work. He had a friend with a furniture shop who asked him to work as a salesman.

When my husband started working for his friend, I went back to school to study cosmetology. I would have preferred to work with computers as I did in Vietnam, but it would have taken three or four years to complete the necessary classes, and I didn't know if I could even get a job. I had two children, and I needed to make a living. The government paid for me to go to cosmetology school, which was great. After I finished with the program and got my license, I found a job in West Hollywood. I worked there for one and one-half years and then moved to another salon in Glendale. After six months, they closed and asked

This picture was taken in France, 2003. This was the first time Thuynga had seen her brother Vu in thirty-eight years and Duy in thirty years. Vu is on the left in the first row, and Duy is on the right in the second row. Thuynga (middle) and her son An (left) are in the second row.

me to come to the Silver Lake store. That was in 1999, and I've been there ever since. I like my job, but language is still an obstacle. Sometimes I want to tell my customers something, but I don't have the words. I don't know what to do. It's very frustrating.

Changes in Vietnam

After fifteen years, I went back to Vietnam to visit family. I felt like an outsider. I noticed that the streets were busier. There were more motorcycles and pollution. I saw that students still study Marx and Engels. Why do they need this? They need to learn about technology, things that will help them. The education is not good. Schools are free now but you still have to pay for some things, and if you pay for those things, it's more like a private school. The second time I went back, I went to the villages. I saw people with nothing, mostly old people and children. Those people able to work had moved to the city to find jobs. Before 1975, there were poor and rich but the distance between them was not as great. Poor people at least had a house, work and food.

Reflections

When we were in Vietnam, we worked to survive. We worked really hard. We worked to have clothes to wear and food to eat. We didn't think about good food like lobster; that wasn't in our minds. We didn't care about beautiful clothes. We just didn't want to be hungry or cold. So when we came here as immigrants, we also worked hard, but for us, that was nothing. We worked six days a week. Some worked seven. We took all the overtime we could get. Maybe that was okay for the first few years when we didn't have anything, but when you have enough, you should set a limit. How many houses and how many cars do you need? I want a simple life. I don't need a castle. I just want a place for my family to live and a car that runs.

In Vietnamese culture, family is the most important thing. Children live with their parents until they are established in a good job. Then they are supposed to take care of their parents when their parents get old. You would never put your aging parents in a nursing home. In fact, nursing homes are nonexistent in Vietnam. I told my children that when I am old, they should put me in a nursing home. I don't want my children to worry about me and my aging issues.

Vietnamese parents are strict with their children. They do not want their children to be out of control. Children have to obey completely even if their parents are wrong. In America, children have too much freedom. Maybe that's because life in America is easier so they are a little more relaxed. Vietnamese children also have respect for their teachers and do whatever they say. Here there is no real respect for teachers. Students talk in the classroom; some stand up and leave. That would never happen in a Vietnamese classroom. I'm not saying that this is the best thing because the problem with the Vietnamese schools is that even if the teachers are wrong, the students must listen and accept what they say. Here the children have an opportunity to speak out and discuss things, and they learn how to be good public speakers.

There is also a big difference between Vietnamese and American women. In America, women have more freedom and rights. They

Thuynga and her husband on Thanksgiving, 2000.

have a high education and good jobs. They are equal to their hubands. You can't be equal when you're a Vietnamese woman. The man is the head of the household. In America, because of the equal standing, women are not subservient. They feel they have an equal say, and that leads to a higher divorce rate. Once you say, "I'm not taking this anymore," there's an easy divorce. Vietnamese women stay in their marriage no matter what happens. If there are problems in the family, we keep them private. We don't have psychologists. Vietnamese people try and put up a perfect image, a perfect family. The problem is that Vietnamese women have to endure a lot more. If your husband becomes a drunk and beats you, you stay with him. You just don't leave him. Even if he has a girlfriend, you turn your head the other way. That would be unheard of for American women. For them it would be "I'm out of here." I think a combination of both would be better, not be too quick to get a divorce but not staying until you're black and blue. I think things are changing; Vietnamese women are starting to follow the lead of American women. More couples are breaking up.

My big dream is for Vietnam to be free and democratic. I want to see an end to communism, and I want to see the education system improve. I want to build our country as one country. Many Vietnamese organizations and individuals here and around the world are trying to help the people who are living in Vietnam. Some focus on children, others on old people, and others on people with disabilities. Some help everyone. Many people gave to me and my family, and I want to give back to my country. I would like to live part of the year here and part of the year in Vietnam. It depends on my family, of course. If my husband or my children need me, I'll stay here. But my goal is to help rebuild my country.

Author

Susan Philips is a Senior Consultant with the Constitutional Rights Foundation (CRF), a national citizenship and law-related educational organization. She also consults with LACER Hollywood Stars, an organization that promotes quality after-school programming in arts, literacy and sports in several middle and high schools. Susan received a Master's degree in Journalism from the University of Southern California and a teaching credential from the University of California at Irvine. This is her second book. *Stepchildren Speak: 10 Grown-up Stepchildren Teach Us How to Build Healthy Stepfamilies*, a collection of interviews with stepchildren, was her first. Susan lives in Los Angeles.